T-Shirts,
MEMORIES
& More™

2013 Indianapolis Colts

Nancy Scott

Annie's®

Meet Nancy Scott

Nancy grew up on a farm in northeastern Indiana, and when not busy with livestock chores, she spent most of her time with her Grandma Scott, who was an avid quilter. On a daily basis, it wasn't unusual to walk into her house and find the kitchen table covered with cardboard templates, fabrics and quilt blocks in progress. At one end of the living room, there was typically a quilting frame set up, and neighbor ladies frequently stopped in to join in the hand stitching.

It was from these beginnings that Nancy developed her love of quilts. She started making her own quilted wall hangings as a teenager and won several awards for her hand quilting while in 4-H.

Fast-forward about 20 years. While Nancy was contemplating a career change, a friend invited her over to "play" on her longarm quilting machine. While it may not have been "love at first stitch," Nancy definitely saw the possibilities. Within a few months she had purchased a longarm quilting machine and started a quilting business, Masterpiece Quilting LLC.

Today Nancy keeps busy making custom and show quilts, quilting for customers and designing quilt patterns.

Introduction

This book is intended to stretch your imagination and your creativity. The goal is to stimulate your thinking and get your creative juices flowing. Rather than a cookie-cutter set of instructions with exact measurements, I've included design techniques and concepts to help you make the most with the T-shirts, clothing, photos and other memory items you have. Each project was designed with flexibility so you can create it your own way.

Memory quilts can include many different items such as clothing, photos and scanned images. They can be used as graduation gifts, as reminders of the baby's days, or as a legacy from those who have passed. Regardless of the way they are used, the purpose remains the same—to fondly recall and reflect upon the memories and stories the items help recall.

The projects in this book are divided into several categories, but by no means are these exclusive. Feel free to substitute a photo where a T-shirt had been placed in the layout, or add a prom dress to a T-shirt quilt. The projects are designed so you can add or subtract rows to make them the size you desire. The Gallery (pages 73–80) showcases a variety of completed projects to give you a launching point. Feel free to be inspired by the layout in one project, the color combinations in another and the addition of photos in a third. Add your own creativity, and it will all come together as something special.

Memory quilts are unique—no two are the same. Just as each person is unique, so are the quilts that commemorate their lives. Don't be afraid to open your mind and your heart when working on a memory quilt. Trust your instincts on what looks or feels right, and allow your creativity to grow.

Table of Contents

Wedding Dress Pillow, page 70

Know the Basics

Preparing the Clothing

Regardless of what type of memory item you are creating, there are some basic steps required to prepare the clothing. Most items will need some kind of stabilizer to keep the fabrics from stretching and to allow them to be cut and stitched together with other types of fabric or memory items.

T-shirts and other washable clothing need to be washed and dried without the use of fabric softener or dryer sheets. The residue from these products is left on the clothes and can interfere with the bond of the fusible stabilizer. If ties or other "dry-clean only" items are excessively dirty, then they should be cleaned. Don't stress over stains on clothing. The stains add character. Boys are proud of the grass stains on their football jerseys. If the stain is offensive, many times it can be worked around in the cutting process.

The Design Process

Create an Inventory

To begin the design process, ask yourself this question: What do I have, and how can I use it?

Sometimes the starting point is the most intimidating. You will frequently be working with irreplaceable items, and you don't want to make a mistake. Yes, it can be rather scary, but with a plan, you can create with confidence. Start by inventorying the items you have to work with while thinking about what you want to create. In many cases this is a pretty straightforward equation. For example, you may have 20 T-shirts, and you want to create a full-size quilt for a high-school graduation present. Or you might have 30 photos, and you want to create a wall hanging for a 25th-anniversary gift. You might have baby clothes and a few photos, and desire to capture the memories in a small lap throw.

In other cases, it's a little more challenging. You could have a box filled with clothing belonging to deceased grandparents and would like to create nine similar items for each of the grandchildren. Regardless of what you have, the design process always starts the same way.

Begin your inventory by sorting your memory items into like groups: jeans, ties, photos, T-shirts, etc. An inventory form has been provided for use with T-shirts on page 15. The form allows you to capture information about color, whether you are using just the front, the back or both the front and back of a shirt. You can measure the heights and widths of the images or logos on the shirts, which will help you determine what size you need to cut each shirt. You can use the information about the width to group like-size T-shirts that may be placed in the same vertical row, or about the height to choose those that might work together in the same horizontal row.

Placement notes are reminders about which shirt needs to be in the center or which could be left out if there are too many. This same form could be easily adapted for use with photos or other items. Filling it out helps you start to organize the project in your mind from the beginning. It also provides you with a checklist that guarantees that an important detail is not forgotten.

What Are You Making?

With an inventory of what you have, start brainstorming about what you want to create. Ask yourself some questions.

• Do you want to make a bed quilt, pillows, a wall hanging, a table runner or something else?

• How big does it need to be? Are there size constraints?

• How will it be used? Will it be a functional bed quilt that's going off to college and will need to be able to withstand daily usage? Or will it be a decorative pillow or wall hanging for a professional office?

• What mood or theme does it need to convey? Is it athletic and fun, or is it dignified and formal? Is it a remembrance of a now-departed loved one or a celebration of a long-married couple?

As you are doing this critical thinking, reflect back on the items you have and start developing a contingency plan if you don't have enough items or too many.

Memory quilts are unique—no two are the same. Just as each person is unique, so are the quilts that reflect her or his life. As you are designing, think about the person or ask lots of questions about the person if you didn't know her or him. If the recipient is a highly professional person, then a more formal and organized or traditional layout may be appropriate. If she or he is an easygoing, fun-loving, spontaneous person, then a less structured, more improvisational pieced quilt may better reflect that sort of personality.

Sketching the Design

By the time you are done with the inventory and brainstorming about the project, it's time to grab some paper and start sketching the design. This can be a simple rough sketch on plain paper or a more formal sketch on graph paper (see Layout Basics on page 11). Your inventory will help you fill in the sizes, and you can make some adjustments to those sizes on the sketch. It helps to have a projected road map of what the project will look like and how you will get there with the materials that you have to work with.

You may have to make several sketches to find the perfect solution for using what you have, in order to end up with the project you want.

Cutting—Making the Most of What You Have

T-Shirts

Start by laying the shirt flat and faceup on a table (Photo 1). Using a pair of sharp shears, cut up the sides to the armpits and then cut the underneath seam on the arm. Cut the shoulder seams open and down the top of the sleeve. You will have two pieces—a front and back with sleeves attached.

Small or X-small T-shirts, where the logo dominates the front of the shirt, require a different cut. For these, lay the shirt facedown and cut up the center back, referring to Photo 2. Cut the shoulder seams open and down the top of the sleeve. Open up the

Cutting Tip

Be sure to put a new blade in your rotary cutter and change it as often as needed. Denim, T-shirts and ties can all dull a blade very quickly.

entire shirt as one piece. This is a very awkward-looking piece, but it will allow you to stabilize a larger area so that you can fussy-cut the logo.

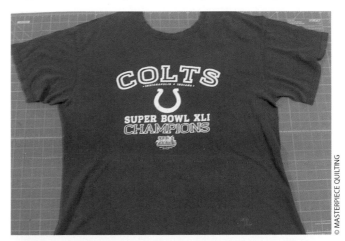

Photo 1

Photo 2

Next do a rough trim on the shirt, cutting approximately 3" below the logo. If you have enough room on the shirt you can trim off the sleeves and along the neckline also (Photo 3).

Photo 3

For long sleeves, cut the sleeves from the shirt at the armhole seam and then remove the cuffs. Cut the seam open under the sleeves to open up the entire sleeve (Photo 4).

Photo 4

For polo-style shirts with a smaller chest logo, it can be challenging to get a cut large enough to use without including the button placket. Until you know exactly how you will be using the logo, give this the same cut as a regular T-shirt but don't trim it.

During this preliminary cutting, save the larger pieces of leftover fabric from the T-shirts since they can be used as pillow backs, strip pillows, as fill-ins for smaller logos and as sashing.

Jeans
Denim jeans are a great source of fabric for memory quilts. How you plan to use the denim determines how you cut up the pants. While deconstructing jeans, use a sharp pair of scissors instead of a rotary cutter.

If you plan to incorporate the back pockets of the pants, you will want to cut them out first. Starting at the back waistband, cut through the waistband and along both sides of the center back seam (Photo 5). Continue cutting down to the crotch seam and stop.

Photo 5

Next, starting at the waistband again, cut along the side seams until you are well below the pocket (Photo 6). When you have cut a large enough area around the pocket, square up the cut toward the center back.

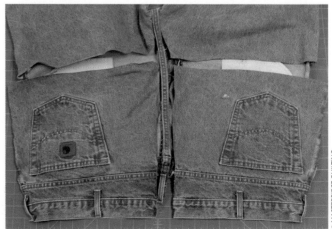

Photo 6

If you want to use long strips or large sections of fabric, separate the jeans into two leg sections. Take a look at the pants and determine whether the inner or outer seam is sewn with a flat-felled seam as shown in Photo 7.

Photo 7

Starting at the bottom of the pant leg, cut on both sides of the flat-felled seam, opening up the leg. Cut as far up as possible and then cut across the leg to create two large pieces of denim with one seam (Photo 8); these can be cut into long strips or larger pieces.

Photo 8

It's best to exclude the flat-felled seam because it is extremely thick and more difficult to sew through when piecing the denim into the quilt.

Ties

Ties can either be used as is, or they can be deconstructed and used similarly to other fabrics. If you use the tie as is, you will need to hand- or machine-appliqué the tie in place with either a topstitch, blanket stitch or some other type of appliqué stitch. Deconstructing the ties gives you more fabric and more options for incorporating the ties into the project.

There is a surprising amount of fabric in a tie. The tie shown in Photo 9A measured 3" wide at the tip, and when deconstructed, it yielded over a 7" width of fabric (Photo 9B).

Photo 9A

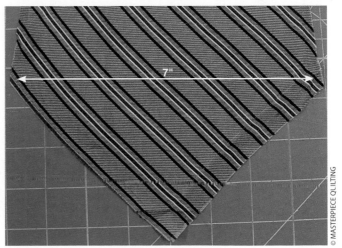

Photo 9B

The process for deconstructing a tie is fairly straight-forward. First, remove any labels and the stitching on the center of the back of the tie (Photo 10).

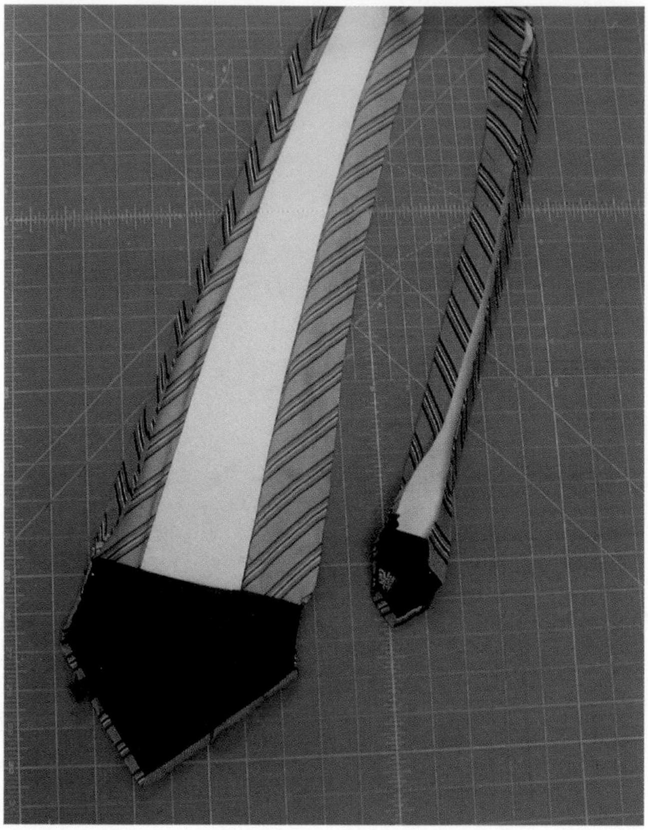

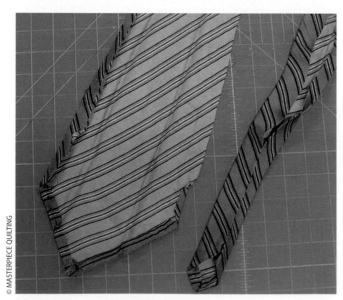

Press the tie on the wrong side using the appropriate setting for the type of fabric in the tie. Many ties are 100 percent silk, while some ties are made from polyester.

Ties are generally constructed from three pieces of fabric as shown in Photo 12. They can either be left stitched together or separated for ease of handling.

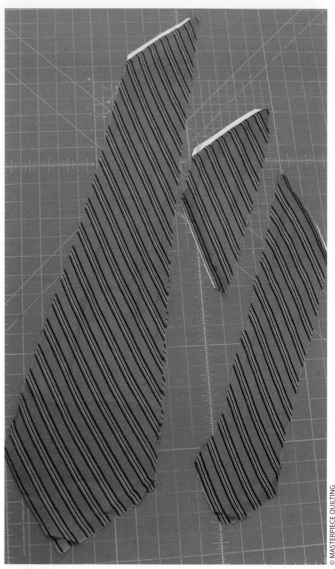

Photo 10

Next, remove and discard the stabilizing fabric. Unstitch and remove the lining fabric from both ends of the tie (Photo 11).

Photo 12

Photo 11

Button-Front Shirts

Button-front shirts are a great source of fabric for memory quilts. They require minimal deconstruction, and you can cut large pieces from them. The sleeves can be deconstructed along the seams to make long strips (Photo 13).

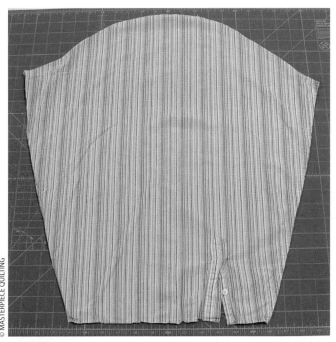

Photo 13

The back can be cut apart to make a large square as shown in Photo 14.

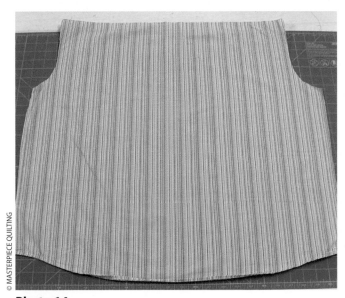

Photo 14

The front side panels can be cut away from the button placket (Photo 15).

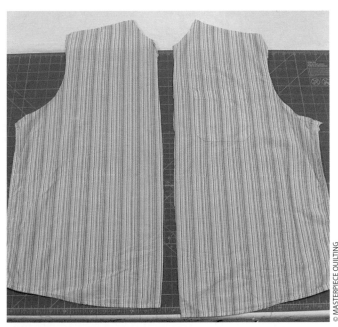

Photo 15

A unique option for pillows is to use the button-up front with buttons and placket left intact for a pillow backing.

To do this, cut the shirt along the side seams, up along the armhole seams, and across the front from shoulder to shoulder (Photo 16).

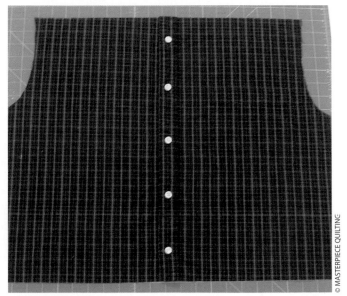

Photo 16

Keeping the buttons buttoned, lay the shirt flat and cut a square or rectangle to match the size needed for a pillow back (Photo 17).

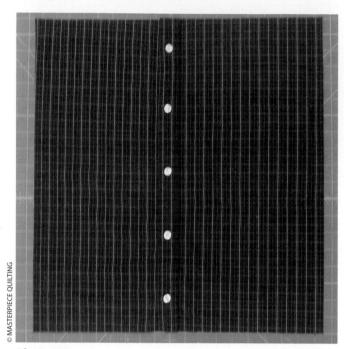

© MASTERPIECE QUILTING

Photo 17

Baby & Children's Clothing
Because of their small size, baby and children's clothing don't yield a lot of fabric from each garment, and each piece is smaller. With this in mind, when using these items in a project, the design will need to be scaled to accommodate the fabric pieces. Most baby clothes have special fasteners that will need to be removed since they can't be sewn through easily. The easiest way to deconstruct baby clothes is to cut along the seams until the clothes lie flat.

Wedding Dresses/Formal Wear
Much like ties, wedding dresses and formal wear are made of specialty fabrics that need special handling. Always press them on the wrong side of the fabric with a dry iron at the correct temperature.

The possibilities are endless when incorporating these fabrics. Shirring, ruffles, lace and beading can all be left intact or cut out and pieced into a memory item. Large pieces of fabric can also be cut from the skirts.

Fabric Photos
Technology has given us lots of options to incorporate photos into memory quilts. The photo can be scanned into a computer and a digital image created. The digital image can then be printed on a photo fabric using a regular ink-jet printer.

There are several types and brands of photo fabric available. These products are backed with paper to facilitate their ability to go through the printer. Follow the manufacturer's directions for best results.

Pictures aren't the only things that can be printed on photo fabric. Text can be printed from a word-processing program. Handwritten documents, wedding invitations and baby announcements are all examples of items that can be scanned and printed to be incorporated into a memory project.

Stabilizing

Why Stabilize?
After you have made the preliminary cuts on the clothing, the next step is to stabilize them with a fusible stabilizer. The stabilizer is used to eliminate the stretch in some fabrics and to provide stability to well-worn clothing.

A wide variety of stabilizers is available. A lightweight iron-on woven stabilizer was used in the projects in this book.

Because many of the fabrics you will be using are already heavy, a lightweight stabilizer provides structure without extra weight or bulk, and it is easier to cut and sew through later. Even though some of the clothing you might use isn't stretch fabric, a more uniform look is achieved if all the fabrics are stabilized. Some fabrics may have only one-way stretch while others may have two-way stretch. Additionally, when cutting the fabric at an angle, you create a bias edge that will stretch further.

How to Use Stabilizer
Follow the stabilizer manufacturer's instructions when applying the iron-on stabilizer. When working with a wide variety of fabrics, you may need to adjust the heat to get a good bond with the stabilizer.

Any new cotton fabric being pieced in with the clothing items does not need to be stabilized.

T-Shirt Quilts

Selecting New Fabric to Add to the Project

When designing a T-shirt quilt or a memory item, try to make sure the T-shirts or the clothing fabrics are the focal point of the quilt. This means keeping other fabric choices and quilting in a secondary or supporting role. For new fabric being added to the quilt, I prefer solids or fabrics that "read" as solids. Many times these are referred to as blender or tonal fabrics (Photo 18).

Photo 18

Batik fabrics are often an excellent choice, with their randomly printed patterns.

Many fabrics are directional, meaning they have a specific top and bottom. When used in a project, the pattern for directional fabrics should be oriented in the correct direction. Even though a T-shirt quilt is really a directional quilt, it is easier not to use directional fabrics for other parts of the quilt. Using them is challenging since you have to be sure to cut and place all the pieces in the proper orientation.

If it fits the theme of the quilt, it's fun to use a novelty fabric, such as a sports print, as an accent, making sure it doesn't compete with the rest of the parts of the quilt. These supporting fabrics help establish the mood of the quilt and make it more personal.

Fabric choices can make a quilt more masculine or feminine, mature or youthful. School colors are perfect for graduation quilts. Bright or bold colors can be selected to match the recipient's personality.

Layout Basics

At this point, you are ready to finalize the layout. One option is to create the layout on paper. It works best to use graph paper to draw the finished size of a block. Add a ¼" seam allowance all around to determine the cut size for the pieces in the block—a 3" finished square would need to be cut 3½" square to include the seam allowance.

Make a second drawing incorporating the blocks into a project layout drawing. Adjust placement of the blocks and determine their exact size along with exact size of the borders and finished quilt.

Another option is to simply begin laying the stabilized pieces on a design wall or on the floor and move them around as needed. This approach is more about trial and error, but it lets you visualize the layout immediately.

Design Tip

A design wall can really help with laying out a quilt. A very simple and economical way to make a design wall is to purchase enough batting or light shade flannel and place on a wall either by tacking into place or making a wooden frame. Your blocks will stick to the batting surface and allow you to lay out your quilt and see how best to arrange them. This will also help with color selection and allow you to make changes if needed before actually stitching the quilt together. You can also purchase design walls ready to use.

Once the layout is firmly established, make the final cuts on the prepared shirts using a rotary cutter with a sharp blade.

Strips cut 2½" wide work well for sashing or framing blocks. These strips finish at 2", which is a nice working width. This size also allows for the use of precut strips. This width gives you enough extra fabric to use as a "fudge factor" to get blocks to fit together correctly.

The sample T-shirt or memory quilts in this book all use 4–6" finished outer borders of cotton fabric. These borders give the finished quilts stability and provide new fabric in the areas that are handled the most—the outer edges.

Construction Guidelines
This book isn't about a lot of rules; rather, it is meant to teach techniques and provide tips that work well in general. Basic sewing construction guidelines should be followed, but not every seam has to be exactly ¼". In some cases a slightly deeper seam works better and takes up extra fabric so blocks fit together.

Pressing is important, and in many cases, it is better to press a seam open to minimize bulk and to make it easier to sew over. Even when fabrics are stabilized, they can still shift as you sew them, so layouts where points don't have to match give you more flexibility in construction and are easiest.

When sewing cotton fabric that has not been stabilized to other stabilized fabrics, it is easier to press the seam toward the cotton. In most cases you will be pressing on the back side of the fabrics. It is important not to press across printed logos on the right side of the fabric because they can smear.

Sewing Tip

Replace your sewing machine needle frequently since denim, T-shirts and ties can all dull the needle quickly. If you are having problems with broken needles, you may need to change needle size, especially when sewing with denim.

Adding Borders
Because no specific size instructions are given for cutting the clothing items for the projects in this book, you will need to figure out the sizes for cutting your borders on your own.

Determine the width of the border strip you want to add. Then measure the vertical length of your quilt from the center of the quilt top to the center of the quilt bottom. This is the size to cut the outer vertical border strips. Unless you are cutting these strips along the length of the fabric, you will have to cut multiple strips to create strips the required length. The strips may be joined with straight or diagonal seams with seams pressed open or to one side.

Once these strips are constructed, they are pinned to the long sides of the quilt, pinning at the top, bottom and center. Add pins in between these pinned areas, easing the edges of the strip and quilt together. Stitch the strips in place, and then press with seams toward the strips.

Repeat this process for the top and bottom strips, measuring from side to side through the quilt center to determine the size to cut these strips.

Finishing

Backing
New cotton fabric is recommended for the back of memory projects as the fabric provides structure and stability. The backing may either be cut from wide fabric made especially for quilt backings, or it may be constructed from fabric-width strips (anywhere from 40"–44" wide) that have been sewn together to create the appropriate size. If you are having your quilt quilted on a longarm machine, it is recommended that the backing be at least 4" larger than the finished top all around. That means the backing for a 60" x 80" finished top should be made 68" x 88".

When seaming pieces for the backing, remove selvage edges and sew the pieces together using a ⅜" seam allowance; press the seam open to distribute bulk. For quilts where the backing might be seen, a novelty print fabric may be used to complement the theme of the quilt.

If someone has a lot of T-shirts, it is not uncommon to piece them into the quilt backing. Consider the following if T-shirts will be used as part of the backing:

1. The quilting stitches will fall at random so custom quilting isn't a good option.

2. The seams on the quilt back need to be staggered so they don't line up with the seams on the top of the quilt; otherwise, the thickness may be too much to stitch through.

Batting

Batting preferences are a personal choice, but low-loft polyester batting is recommended for use in clothing quilts for several reasons. Polyester has minimal-to-no shrinkage, so the quilt won't pucker when it's washed and dried. It is also very lightweight. This is especially important with larger quilts that can already be heavy from the weight of the fabrics. Finally, polyester batting is very easy to care for. It can be laundered in a regular washing machine and can go straight into a dryer with no special attention.

Quilting a T-Shirt/Clothing Quilt

T-shirt quilts are typically quilted with an edge-to-edge or allover pattern. These type of patterns start with stitching on one side of the quilt and continue to the opposite side without regard to the placement of the T-shirts. These patterns can be very simple in design to allow the T-shirts to be the focal point. Many times the pattern reflects the theme of the quilt such as sports or music. Custom quilting is another option for T-shirt quilts where the quilting pattern echoes around the logos printed on the T-shirts.

If you are hand-quilting, tying or quilting the quilt on your home machine, sandwich the batting between the quilt top and the prepared backing; pin or baste layers together to hold. Quilt or tie as desired, keeping layers flat.

When quilting or tying is complete, trim excess batting and backing even with the edges of the quilt top to prepare for binding.

Binding

Binding finishes the edges of a quilted project. A double-layered binding is recommended.

To determine how much binding is needed, measure the distance around your quilt and add 12". Strips will need to be cut and joined with diagonal seams to create one strip this length for binding.

For the quilts in this book, binding strips were cut 2½" across the straight grain of the fabric. To join

one or more strips to obtain the desired length, use diagonal seams to distribute the bulk. Trim the seams to ¼" and press open (Figure 1).

Figure 1

Cut one end of the binding strip at a 45-degree angle and fold a ¼" hem to the wrong side and press. Fold the entire strip in half lengthwise with wrong sides together and press (Figure 2).

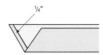

Figure 2

Position the binding along one edge of the quilted project, matching the raw edges of the binding and the quilted top. Begin stitching 3" from the binding end, using a ¼" seam allowance. Stitch to within ¼" of the first corner and then sew diagonally to the point of the corner (Figure 3).

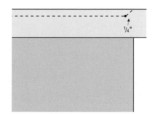

Figure 3

Clip threads and remove the piece from the machine. Fold the binding up at a 45-degree angle to the seam (Figure 4) and back down even with the quilt edge, forming a pleat at the corner (Figure 5). Resume stitching down the next side, going around each corner in the same manner.

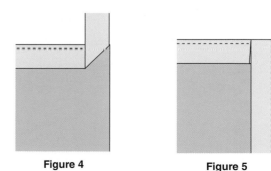

Figure 4   **Figure 5**

Stop sewing the binding a short distance from the beginning tail of binding. Trim the end tail of the binding so that it tucks inside the beginning tail at least 2". Finish stitching (Figure 6).

Figure 6

Turn the folded edge of the binding to the back of the project and stitch in place by hand or machine. The corners will naturally fold into a miter; use a few hand stitches to secure the miter fold.

Finishing Touches—Labels & Embellishments

After the quilting and binding are completed, embellishments may be hand-sewn onto the item. These are items that would interfere with or could get damaged in the construction and quilting processes such as letter-jacket patches, medallions, Scout patches and hair bows.

Before the quilt is considered finished, be sure to create and apply a label to the back of the quilt. Include information about who it was made for, who it was made by, when it was made, and any other special information about the memory items. ■

Professional Quilting

If you currently use the services of a professional quilter, check with her or him in advance to find out how she or he might handle T-shirt or memory quilts. Not all quilters are willing to stitch this type of quilt. Check to see if there are any restrictions regarding embellishments, buttons, etc., along with the sizes of backing and batting that will be required.

Inventory Form

T-Shirt Description	Color	Front? Back? Both? Seamed?	Logo Width	Logo Height	Placement

Traditional Square Blocks With Four Sashing Options

It is easy to change the look of a T-shirt quilt by using different sashing treatments. Each T-shirt is cut into a 15½" square and the same shirts will be used for each example. Nine T-shirts stitched together in three rows of three blocks each were used in the sample. This size makes a beautiful throw-size quilt and is a perfect project for an inexperienced quilter.

Specifications
Skill Level: Beginner
Sample Quilt Size: 61" x 61"

Materials
- 9 T-shirts
- Fabric for sashings, borders and binding
- Batting to size
- Backing to size
- Thread
- Fusible stabilizer
- Basic sewing tools and supplies

Preparing the T-Shirts
1. Prepare T-shirts with fusible stabilizer as directed on page 10 of the Know the Basics section.

2. Center the logos and cut each T-shirt into a 15½" square.

3. Arrange the squares in a pleasing configuration. *Note: Four different sashing options using the same set of T-shirt squares are presented to illustrate how the quilt appearance changes as certain design elements change.*

Traditional Squares With Plain Sashing
In this example, the sashing strips are all cut from one fabric and finish at 3" wide. The border finishes at 5" wide and is cut from a second color fabric. Remember that you should choose sashing and border widths that work with the size of your T-shirt squares and the predetermined finished size of the quilt.

1. To achieve this look, cut six 3½" x 15½" sashing strips.

2. Arrange and join the sashing strips with the T-shirt squares to make block rows referring to the Assembly Diagram; press seams toward strips.

3. Measure the width of the row and cut two long horizontal sashing strips at 3½" by this length.

4. Join the block rows with horizontal sashing strips to complete the quilt top referring to the Assembly Diagram; press seams toward strips.

5. Measure the quilt top to determine border sizes and prepare 5½"-wide side border strips referring to page 12 of Know the Basics.

6. Sew the side border strips in place; press seams toward the strips.

7. Repeat steps 5 and 6 to add the top and bottom borders.

8. Layer, quilt and bind edges referring to pages 12–13 of Know the Basics to finish the quilt.

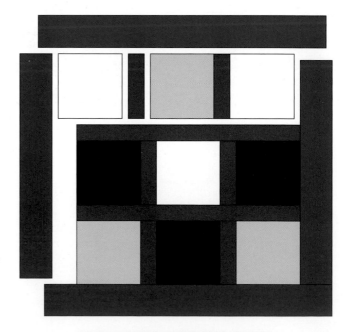

Traditional Squares With Plain Sashing
Assembly Diagram 61" x 61"

Traditional Squares With Cornerstone Sashing

In this example, the T-shirt squares remain the same but the horizontal sashing strips are separated into sashing strips and cornerstone squares. The sashing strips run between the blocks and the cornerstone squares are at the corners where the sashes meet. The sashing strips are cut 3½" wide and the outer border strips are cut 5½" wide. The sashes are one color, the cornerstone squares another color, and the border is yet another. You can see how the look of the quilt has changed with just the addition of the cornerstones.

1. To complete this layout, cut 12 sashing strips at 3½" x 15½" from one fabric and four 3½" cornerstone squares from a contrasting fabric.

2. Arrange the T-shirt squares, sashing strips and cornerstone squares on a flat surface referring to the Assembly Diagram.

3. Sew the sashing strips between the T-shirt squares to create block rows referring to Figure 1; press seams toward sashing strips.

Make 3

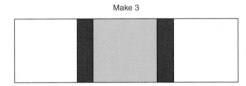

Figure 1

Traditional Squares With Cornerstone Sashing
Assembly Diagram 61" x 61"

4. Join the horizontal sashing strips and cornerstone squares to create sashing rows as shown in Figure 2; press seams toward the sashing strips.

Make 2

Figure 2

5. Join the block rows and sashing rows referring to the Assembly Diagram; press seams toward the sashing rows.

6. Add outer borders referring to steps 5–7 of Traditional Squares With Plain Sashing.

7. Layer, quilt and bind edges referring to pages 12–13 of Know the Basics to finish the quilt.

Traditional Squares With Friendship Star Sashing

The Friendship Star is the name of a traditional quilt block. It is very easy to add Friendship Stars to the sashing and cornerstones to create the star design. The T-shirts remain the same, as does the width of the sashing and borders in the previous examples. The sashes are one color, and the cornerstones and stars points are a second color to provide contrast. The addition of the stars gives the quilt an entirely new look.

1. Cut 12 (3½" x 15½") sashing strips from one fabric and 20 (3½" x 3½") cornerstone and star-point squares from a contrasting-color fabric.

2. Draw a diagonal line on the wrong side of 16 of the 3½" squares.

3. Place a marked square right sides together at the end of a sashing strip and sew on the marked line. Trim the seam to ¼" and press the stitched piece to the right side to create a star point as shown in Figure 3. Repeat on the remaining sashing strips.

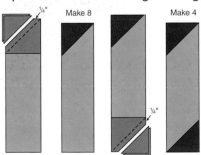

Figure 3

4. Repeat step 3 to add a second marked square on the remaining end of four sashing strips, again referring to Figure 3.

5. Arrange the sashing strips and T-shirt squares in three rows of three blocks each with sashing strips between referring to the Assembly Diagram.

6. Sew three T-shirt blocks with two stitched sashing strips as arranged to make a block row; press seams toward the sashing strips. Repeat to make three block rows.

7. Join three sashing strips as arranged to make a sashing row; press seams toward the strips. Repeat to make as second sashing row.

8. Join the block rows and sashing rows referring to the Assembly Diagram; press seams toward the sashing rows.

9. Add outer borders referring to steps 5–7 of Traditional Squares With Plain Sashing.

10. Layer, quilt and bind edges referring to pages 12 and 13 of Know the Basics to finish the quilt.

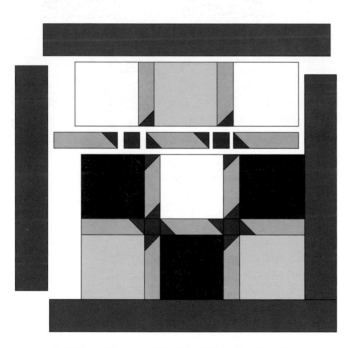

Traditional Squares With Friendship Star Sashing
Assembly Diagram 61" x 61"

Traditional Squares With 8-Point Star Sashing

The 8-Point Star is another traditional quilt design. It is a little more difficult than the Friendship Star but it will give a very polished look to your quilt. Like the Friendship Star, the 8-Point Star is an extension of the cornerstone squares. The T-shirts remain the same size as does the width of the sashing and borders. The sashing strips are one color and the cornerstone squares and star points are another color to provide contrast.

1. To complete this layout, cut 12 (3½" x 15½") sashing strips from one fabric. Cut four 3½" x 3½" cornerstone squares and 32 (2" x 2") star-point squares from a contrasting-color fabric.

2. Draw a diagonal line from corner to corner on the wrong side of each 2" square.

3. Place a marked square right sides together on one corner of a sashing strip and sew on the marked line; trim the seam to ¼" and press the piece to the right side as shown in Figure 4.

Figure 4

4. Place a second marked square on the adjacent corner of the same end of the sashing strip and sew along the marked line; trim seam to ¼" and press the piece to the right side to complete a strip/star-point unit as shown in Figure 5.

Figure 5

5. Repeat steps 3 and 4 with the remaining sashing strips and marked 2" squares to complete a total of 12 strip/star-point units.

6. Select four strip/star-point units and repeat steps 3 and 4 on the opposite end of each to make four center strip/star-point units referring to Figure 6.

Make 4

Figure 6

7. Arrange and join three T-shirt squares with two strip/star-point units to make a block row referring to the Assembly Diagram; press seams open to reduce bulk. Repeat to make a second block row.

8. Arrange and join three T-shirt squares with two center strip/star-point units to make the center block row; press seams open.

9. Arrange and join two strip/star-point units with a center strip/star-point unit to make a sashing row; press seams open to reduce bulk. Repeat to make a second sashing row.

10. Join the block rows with the sashing rows to complete the quilt center; press seams open to distribute bulk.

11. Add outer borders referring to steps 5–7 of Traditional Squares With Plain Sashing.

12. Layer, quilt and bind edges referring to pages 12 and 13 of Know the Basics to finish the quilt. ∎

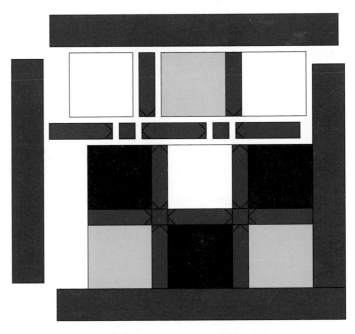

Traditional Squares With 8-Point Star Sashing
Assembly Diagram 61" x 61"

Framed T-Shirt Quilt

Instead of cutting all the T-shirts the same size, this layout allows you to custom-cut each shirt based on the size of the logo. Add sashing to create a staggered look to the quilt. This is an excellent layout to use when you don't have quite enough shirts to make a certain size quilt because of the additional fabric added around each block. Because the shirts are trimmed close to the logo, this layout allows you to incorporate more T-shirts in your quilt and allows your eye to focus on the logos. The sample quilt features T-shirts purchased on vacations. The mood of the quilt is fun and lively, and the bright batik border adds to that feeling.

Specifications
Skill Level: Beginner
Sample Quilt Size: 67" x 80"

Materials
- T-shirts
- Fabric for sashings, borders and binding
- Backing to size
- Batting to size
- Thread
- Fusible stabilizer
- Basic sewing tools and supplies

Preparing the T-Shirts
1. Record the T-shirt information on a copy of the inventory sheet located on page 15.

2. Prepare T-shirts with fusible stabilizer as directed on page 10 of the Know the Basics section. To make the same size as the sample quilt, you will need 14 adult-size T-shirts.

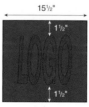

3. Referring to Figure 1, trim the T-shirts at least 1½" from the top and bottom of the logo. Center the logo and cut the T-shirts 15½" wide.

Figure 1

Here's a Tip
Select sashing strips in colors to convey a theme. Dark-color strips would be appropriate for a man-cave quilt while bright-color strips would be perfect for a younger child. Make the selection based on the theme of the T-shirts or to tie the shirts together into cohesive group.

Completing the Quilt Top
In this example, the sashing strips join the T-shirt blocks into vertical rows. Each vertical row in the sample is the same width, but the rows could be different widths.

1. To achieve this look, cut 2½" by fabric width sashing strips in a variety of colors. You will need two same-fabric strips for most blocks.

2. Measure the vertical sides of a T-shirt block, select a 2½"-wide strip and cut two strips the measured length.

3. Sew the two cut strips to the vertical sides of the T-shirt block as shown in Figure 2; press seams toward the strips.

Figure 2

4. Measure the horizontal sides of the stitched unit and cut two more strips this same length from the remainder of the strip cut in step 2 and the second same-color strip, if necessary. Sew these strips to the top and bottom of the T-shirt block as shown in Figure 3; press seams toward the strips.

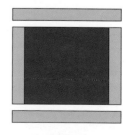

Figure 3

5. Repeat steps 2–4 for all T-shirt blocks.

6. Arrange the framed blocks in vertical rows referring to the Assembly Diagram and the photo below for positioning suggestions. Adjust row lengths by trimming sashings as necessary to make rows.

7. Sew the rows together; press seams open.

8. Measure the quilt top to determine border sizes and prepare 5½"-wide side border strips referring to page 12 of Know the Basics.

9. Sew the side border strips in place; press seams toward the strips.

10. Repeat steps 8 and 9 to add the top and bottom borders.

11. Layer, quilt and bind edges referring to pages 12 and 13 of Know the Basics to finish the quilt. ∎

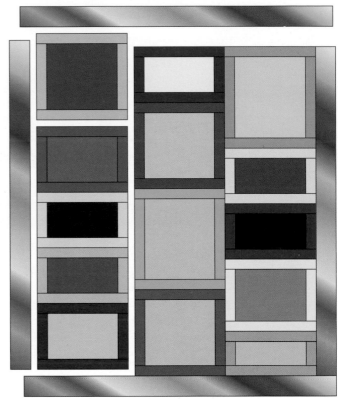

Framed T-Shirt Quilt
Assembly Diagram 67" x 80"

60-Degree Triangle T-Shirt Quilt

The sample 60-Degree Triangle T-Shirt Quilt is an example of how smaller logos from button/collared shirts or T-shirts can be used to make an interesting quilt. It's easy to center and cut the logo using a 60-degree triangle tool (Photo 1).

Specifications
Skill Level: Intermediate
Sample Quilt Size: 55¼" x 49"

Materials
- T-shirts
- Fabric for setting triangles, borders and binding
- Backing to size
- Batting to size
- Thread
- Fusible stabilizer
- 8" finished 60-degree clear triangle tool
- Basic sewing tools and supplies

Preparing the T-Shirts
1. Prepare T-shirts with fusible stabilizer as directed on page 10 of the Know the Basics section, leaving the plackets in place. In some cases you may need to unstitch part of the placket in order to get a nice layout. Try to avoid using the placket if at all possible since it is stiff, bulky and difficult to stitch through. For this quilt you need 23 logo motifs.

2. Referring to Photo 2, center the 60-degree triangle over the logo on each shirt front. Without moving the shirt, fussy-cut around the triangle

Photo 1

using a rotary cutter as shown in the photo. ***Note:*** *You may trace around the triangle, remove the triangle and then cut out with shears, if desired.*

Completing the Quilt Top
In this example, the logo triangles are joined together alternately with same-size triangles of a coordinating batik fabric. The batik has multiple shades of green/white/gold and blends well with the logo triangle colors.

1. Using the same 60-degree triangle ruler, cut triangles and half triangles as needed for the setting triangles. ***Note:*** *The sample shown uses 22 whole triangles and five each half triangles and reversed half triangles.*

2. Arrange the logo triangles, setting triangles, half triangles and reversed half triangles in horizontal rows referring to the Assembly Diagram. When satisfied with the arrangement, join the triangles to make rows; press seams away from the logo triangles referring to arrows in Figure 1.

Figure 1

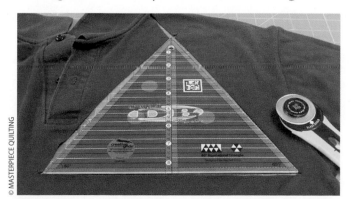

Photo 2

l stop.

3. Join the rows, matching triangle points as shown in Figure 2, to complete the quilt center; press row-joining seams open to reduce bulk. ***Note:*** *See Matching Triangle Points in Seams sidebar on next page for more information about matching the points.*

Figure 2

4. Measure the quilt top to determine border sizes and prepare 5"-wide top and bottom border strips referring to page 12 of Know the Basics.

5. Sew the top and bottom border strips in place; press seams toward the strips.

6. Repeat steps 4 and 5 to add the side borders.

7. Layer, quilt and bind edges referring to pages 12 and 13 of Know the Basics to finish the quilt. ■

Here's a Tip

If your T-shirts are too small to stabilize before cutting, center and cut the logo triangles, add stabilizer to the back of the triangles and trim again to guarantee that the triangles will all be the same size. They will stretch out of shape a little when applying stabilizer, so the second trimming will be necessary to guarantee an accurate size for the constructions steps.

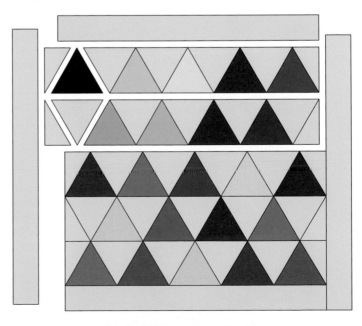

60-Degree Triangle T-Shirt Quilt
Assembly Diagram 55¼" x 49"

T-Shirts, Memories & More

Matching Triangle Points in Seams

When joining rows of triangles such as 60-degree triangles, the direction the seams are pressed becomes very important.

When triangles are joined to make rows, it is important that the joining seams in adjoining rows be pressed in opposite directions. In the sample quilt shown, a logo triangle is joined with a setting triangle, and the seams are always pressed toward the setting triangle. When joining the rows, the seams will already be pressed in opposite directions because the triangles are alternated in the rows.

To stitch, align one triangle point with another and place a pin through the exact points, keeping seams pressed in opposite directions.

Trim the excess triangle points beyond the seams as shown in Figure A. You may also want to trim some of the overlapped seam allowance where the seams were pressed toward the setting triangles as shown in Figure B.

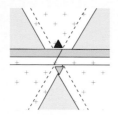

Figure A

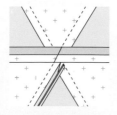

Figure B

If you would like to guarantee that this seam does not move around when stitching the rows, simply stitch a 1" line of basting stitches through the point as shown in Figure C, removing the pin only when you get to it.

Figure C

Open and check that the points still match after stitching, referring to Figure D; if not, remove basting and try again. Repeat this process on each point.

Figure D

Now you are ready to stitch the rows together with perfect matching triangle points.

Cluster T-Shirt Quilt With T-Shirt Border Option

Of all the T-shirt layouts in this book, the cluster layout is the most complex. It is essentially a collage of T-shirts and sashing fabric. The assembly isn't in rows and columns; it is in sections. Many times, when looking at a cluster-layout quilt, it is difficult to determine exactly how it was sewn together. An advantage of the cluster layout is that you can put a lot of shirts into the quilt because you are trimming very close to the logos. The theme of the sample quilt is college athletics. The solid black sashing gives it a very masculine feel and allows the clusters to stand out.

Specifications

Skill Level: Intermediate
Sample Quilt Size: 67" x 79"

Materials

- T-shirts
- Fabric for sashings, borders and binding
- Backing to size
- Batting to size
- Thread
- Fusible stabilizer
- Basic sewing tools and supplies

Preparing the T-Shirts

1. Record the T-shirt information on a copy of the inventory sheet located on page 15.

2. Prepare T-shirts with fusible stabilizer as directed on page 10 of the Know the Basics section. Trim each shirt close to the logos to eliminate blank space. ***Note:*** *See Trimming Logos to Size sidebar on page 30 for more information.*

Completing the Quilt Center

1. Arrange the T-shirt blocks on a design wall or flat surface (see photo at left). Move around to group in similar-size clusters and find the best combinations.

2. Cut sashing strips to add between blocks when joining to make cluster units of similar widths or heights. The sample quilt uses 1½"–3" sashing strips as needed to make the blocks work together.

3. Join two similar-size blocks with a sashing strip as shown in Figure 1. Trim the unit as necessary to make the edges match. Press seams toward the sashing strip.

Figure 1

Here's a Tip

A design wall is very helpful when auditioning the T-shirt blocks for placement. It helps to be able to move around and view the blocks in different placements. It also helps to be able to arrange blocks according to size.

28

4. Repeat step 3 with two more similar-size T-shirt blocks and sashing strip, trimming blocks as necessary to make the edges match.

5. Join these two cluster units with a sashing strip and trim to make the edges match as shown in Figure 2 to complete one cluster.

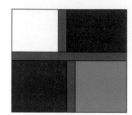

Figure 2

6. Repeat steps 3–5 to make a second cluster the same width as the previously pieced cluster as shown in Figure 3.

Figure 3

7. Arrange the clusters on the design wall, separating where a sashing strip will be added, referring to Figure 4.

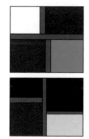

Figure 4

Here's a Tip

If you have a design wall, take advantage of your digital camera to take a photo of each layout audition. You are sure to find a favorite based on color and size when you view all of your choices side by side.

8. Measure the width of cluster groups for sashing strip length needed to join the two clusters to make a row referring to Figure 5 as an example. Cut a 2½"-wide sashing strip this length.

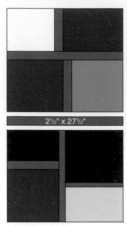

2½" x 27½"

Figure 5

Trimming Logos to Size

As a general rule, trim at least 1½" away from the top, bottom and sides of a logo for a cluster layout. This allows you to incorporate more shirts in the quilt than a traditional layout.

Record the measurements of the cut logos on the inventory form given on page 15. Using these measurements, sort out shirts that are the same height or the same width. These shirts can easily be sewn together with sashing into clusters. At this time, I start sketching the layout on paper, grouping like-size shirts.

For planning purposes, I factor in a 2" finished sashing strip between the shirts but this can easily be trimmed smaller if needed.

Lay out the blocks in a staggered fashion so the seams don't match from one row to the next. Scatter the blocks around to get nice color distribution.

9. Join the clusters with the sashing strip referring to Figure 6 to complete the first cluster row; press seams toward the sashing strip.

Figure 6

10. Arrange and join the larger T-shirt blocks in one vertical and one horizontal row. Add sashing strips to make the vertical row match the height of the first cluster row. Referring to the Assembly Diagram, join the vertical row to the first cluster row with a sashing strip. Press seams toward the sashing strips.

11. Measure the width of the joined rows and add sashing strips to the horizontal row to match this measurement. Referring to the Assembly Diagram, join the horizontal row to the bottom of the previous rows with a sashing strip. Press seams toward the sashing strips.

12. To complete the quilt center, measure the quilt top to determine inner border sizes and prepare 2½"-wide inner border strips referring to page 12 of Know the Basics. Add an inner border to the bottom edge first, then the sides and then add the top inner border, referring to the Assembly Diagram on page 32; press seams toward inner border strips.

Adding T-Shirt Borders

1. Measure the quilt top to determine T-shirt border sizes referring to page 12 of Know the Basics.

2. Center the logos and cut T-shirts into rectangles. *Note: The sample used rectangles cut 9½" from top to bottom, but in different sizes from side to side.*

3. Audition the T-shirt blocks on the sides and bottom of the quilt with the logo upright on the bottom and placed vertically on the sides as shown in Figure 7 so that they can be read when the quilt is on the bed and these borders hang down on the sides.

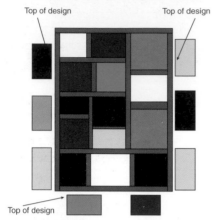

Figure 7

4. Cut sashing strips 9½" wide by the lengths needed to create a strip the length of the long sides of the quilt top.

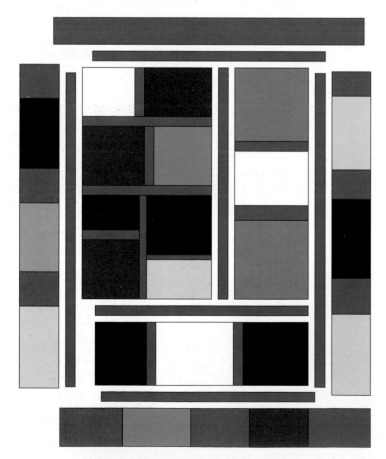

Cluster T-Shirt Quilt With T-Shirt Border Option
Assembly Diagram 67" x 79"

5. Join the sashing strips with the T-shirt blocks, trimming excess at ends as necessary referring to the Assembly Diagram for positioning of these strips; press seams toward the sashing strips.

6. Sew the side T-shirt borders to opposite sides of the quilt center, arranging so that the top of the logos are against the quilt center referring to the Assembly Diagram; press seams toward the inner borders.

7. Measure the bottom edge of the bordered quilt top and cut 9½" wide sashing strips in the lengths required to make a strip this length when stitched with the blocks.

8. Join the strips and the T-shirt blocks to make the bottom T-shirt border referring to the Assembly Diagram for positioning; press seams toward the sashing strips. Trim border to the exact size needed for the bottom T-shirt border, if necessary.

9. Sew this border to the bottom of the bordered quilt center; press seam toward the inner border

10. Prepare a 5½"-wide border strip referring to page 12 of Know the Basics and sew to the top edge of the bordered quilt center.

11. Layer, quilt and bind edges referring to pages 12 and 13 of Know the Basics to finish the quilt. ■

Here's a Tip

Half the battle of making the clusters work is knowing the block sizes needed before you start sewing. Drawing a sketch on paper with the sizes is helpful. In the end, the blocks need to fit together to make the cluster units and the units have to be joined to create a larger cluster.

To accomplish this, size matters! Some quilters like to plan these sizes from the start, while others like to work by the seat of their pants and trim or add borders to adjust the size.

Use whatever method works for you to reach your goal of a quilt that is the same size on both side lengths and on the top and bottom lengths before adding borders.

T-Shirt Orientation

In the sample quilt, careful planning is required to guarantee that the orientation of the T-shirt blocks in the outer borders allows for the quilt to hang over the sides and bottom of the bed while still being able to read the information on the shirts.

To make a quilt like this, you must know the size of the bed on which the quilt will be used so that the outer borders will end up hanging over the sides of the bed.

Plain borders were added to the sides of the pieced center on the sample quilt to adjust the finished size to fit across the top of the bed and allow for the addition of the blocks that would hang over the sides.

The top edge of the quilt does not need special treatment except to add a border strip as a finish.

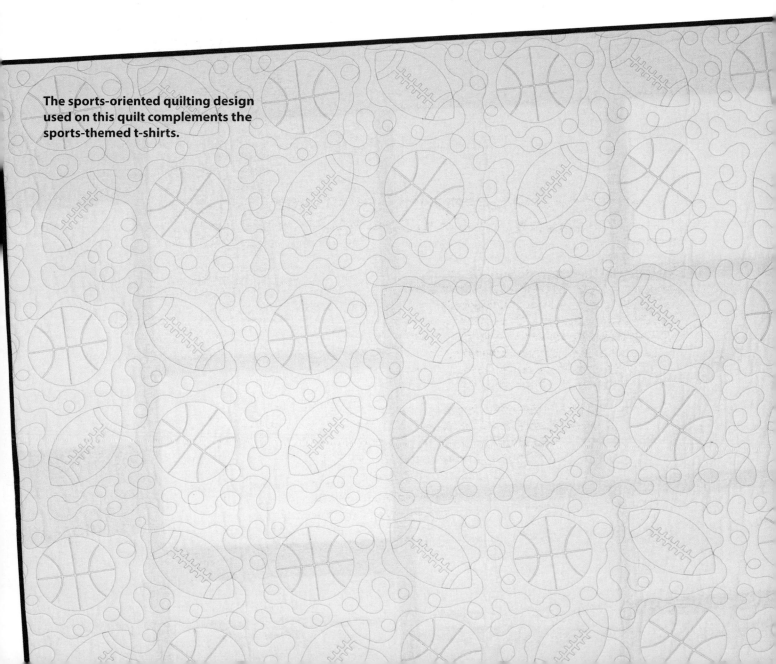

The sports-oriented quilting design used on this quilt complements the sports-themed t-shirts.

Clothing Sampler Quilt

Take recycling to new levels while preserving memories in a quilt using scraps from one or more person's clothing. The sample quilt shown was created from women's clothing and includes a variety of different block options. The same quilt could also be created using men's clothing, kids' clothing or baby clothing. The sashing can either be made from clothing or new fabric. In the quilt shown, old shirts were used for the sashing, and only the outer border and binding were made with new fabric. Instead of using only one block for the entire quilt, this quilt uses four different options for creating blocks. These four include fussy-cut blocks, Four-Patch blocks, Nine-Patch blocks and Crazy-Patch blocks. You can mix and match these however you like or create a quilt with just one block of your choice.

Specifications
Skill Level: Beginner
Sample Quilt Size: 50" x 50"

Materials
- Clothing items
- Fabric for sashings, borders and binding
- Backing to size
- Batting to size
- Thread
- Fusible stabilizer
- Basic sewing tools and supplies

Design Decisions
This type of quilt requires a greater level of design decisions before beginning. Start by looking through the clothing items and, if needed, prepare an inventory list similar to the one used with T-shirt quilts to start organizing what you have.

Sort out any pieces of clothing that have patterns that could be fussy-cut. This includes clothing with large floral patterns, embroidery and other motifs. Fussy cutting allows you to center a design and keep a larger portion of the piece of clothing together (Photo 1).

© MASTERPIECE QUILTING

Photo 1

Select a new fabric to be used for the border and binding. Since the clothing in the sample represented an older woman, and there were quite a few items with floral patterns, a floral print fabric that contained many of the colors found in the clothes was chosen for the borders and binding as seen in the project photo on page 38. Many clothing items may be faded from wear, so the border fabric could be used to brighten up the quilt.

Next, select several pieces of clothing that could be used for the sashing pieces. Work backward to lay out the sashing fabrics first.

After adding several blocks, step back from the layout; take a good look at it and ask some critical design questions:

- Do the colors balance?
- Are there two of the same fabrics touching each other?
- Does the layout look visually appealing?
- Am I missing one of the shirts?

As you continue to cut up the shirts, obviously the remaining pieces keep getting smaller. Smaller motifs can be cut into smaller squares to be used in pieced blocks. In the sample quilt, squares in the Four-Patch block were cut at 3½" and sewn together as shown in Photo 2. Some embroidered sections of a garment were used in one of the sample blocks.

© MASTERPIECE QUILTING

Photo 2

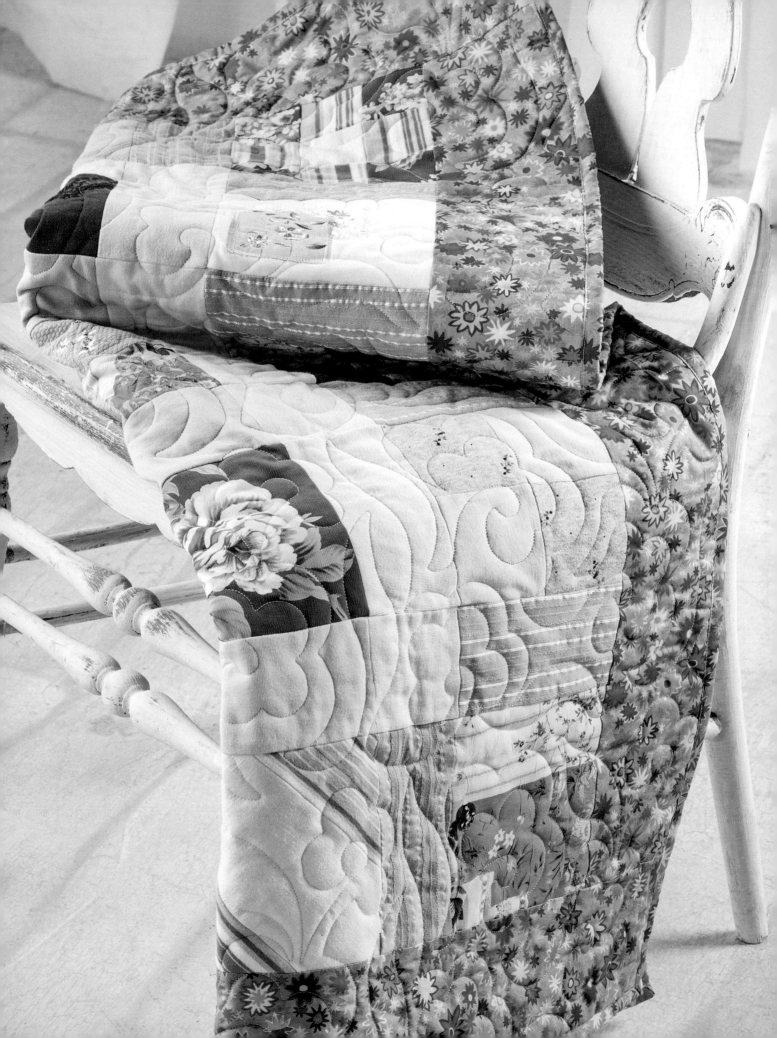

After making several Four-Patch blocks, try making some Nine-Patch blocks using even smaller pieces of clothing (Photo 3). The squares in the Nine-Patch block in the sample were cut 2½" square.

© MASTERPIECE QUILTING

Photo 3

Finally, you may decide to make some improvisational pieced or Crazy-Patch blocks from the remaining sections of clothing.

While sorting through the clothes, create a sample layout in your mind. If you know that the size of the end product is to be a throw, that gives you a finished-size range. You could use the size of the project shown (50" x 50") as a guide, or you could aim for another size depending on the projected use of the quilt and how many clothing items you have from which to choose fabrics.

In order for the blocks to blend cohesively, it makes sense to make the blocks all the same size. The blocks for this sample finish at 6" square. The sashing size is half that size, or a 3" finished width. A 4" finished border all around is a good finish for this size quilt.

Before you begin, it helps to sketch out the layout of the quilt on paper. This could be on a plain piece of paper using a rough sketch or a more precise drawing on graph paper. This drawing will be a pattern for layout and sizes to cut pieces for sashing. Figure 1 shows a computer

sketch of the layout for this sample quilt. It has sizes filled in for cutting the sashing and shows the placement of the blocks and sashing. Some quilters are comfortable with stitching and then planning, while others like to be precise right from the beginning.

These instructions give you the sizes to cut to make each of the blocks with some general instructions for piecing those blocks. They include cutting instructions for sashing strips as used in the sample quilt. You may use these instructions as a springboard to leap into creating your own design based on the materials you have on hand.

The sample quilt uses a variety of clothing types. Striped shirts were used so they could be fussy-cut to take advantage of their striped patterns to provide more visual interest. Large floral designs, embroidered flowers and more were chosen from the clothing items. It's time for you to get started!

Preparing the Clothing Items
1. Stabilize the chosen clothing items referring to page 10 of Know the Basics.

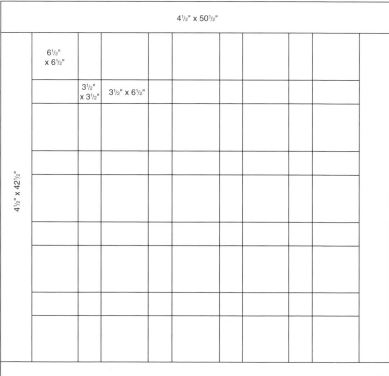

Figure 1

2. Sort the items into piles to be used as sashing, fussy-cut squares or items that are to be cut into smaller pieces to be used in the pieced blocks.

Making Fussy-Cut Squares
1. Select the clothing items from the stack set aside to be fussy-cut.

2. Refer to the Fussy Cutting sidebar on page 40 to create the fussy-cut squares. *Note: The sample quilt has 11 of these fussy-cut squares, each 6½".*

Cutting the Sashing Pieces
The sashing pieces were cut next for the sample quilt. The sashing squares were all cut from one fabric while the sashing strips were cut from several fabrics, including striped fabrics. Having a visual layout really helps with this type of quilt. This layout can either be auditioned on a design wall or on a floor, bed or table.

1. Select the clothing item from which you will cut the sashing squares. For the quilt shown, you will need to cut 16 (3½") squares.

2. Select the clothing items from which you will cut the sashing strips. For the quilt shown, you will need 40 (3½" x 6½") sashing rectangles—16 of the first color (medium blue in the sample), 12 of the second color (green in the sample), eight of the third color (light blue in the sample) and four of the final color (stripe in the sample).

3. Arrange the sashing strips and sashing squares, and insert the fussy-cut squares where you want them to be placed referring to Figure 2.

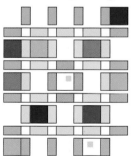

Figure 2

Making Four-Patch Blocks
A Four-Patch block is made up of four same-size squares. Most often there are two sets of two matching squares joined to offset the colors as shown in Figure 3.

Figure 3

1. Select two clothing items from which to cut the squares.

2. Cut two (3½") squares each from the two different clothing items. *Note: Fussy-cut two of the squares if you have smaller motifs to showcase.*

3. Arrange and join the squares into two rows of two squares each to make two pieced rows referring to Figure 4; press seams toward the darker fabric.

4. Join the rows to complete one Four-Patch block, again referring to Figure 4.

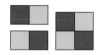

Figure 4

5. Repeat steps 1–4 to complete four Four-Patch blocks.

6. Place these blocks into the blank spaces of your arrangement.

Making Nine-Patch Blocks
Nine-Patch blocks contain nine same-size squares in three rows of three squares each. Usually four squares are of the same fabric and five squares are of a second fabric. These two groups should have some contrast so that a design is created. It can be either four dark and five light, or four light and five

Here's a Tip
Because the clothing items are stabilized, even very stretchy double-knits and other unusual fabrics that are not normally combined in sewing or quilting can be used in this type of memory quilt. Be careful when combining elegant dress materials with other fabrics if the quilt will be washed. If a clothing item has never been washed, it would be a good idea to test It to see if the color will run and if it will shrink. This type of quilt is made to be used and that means it will be laundered. You want to be sure that the fabrics used in the quilt will stand up to wear and tear, and will still survive the washer and dryer.

dark as shown in Figure 5. In really scrappy quilts, all squares can be cut from different fabrics and no pattern is created. In the sample quilt, both of the patterned versions are used.

Figure 5

1. Select two clothing items to be used in one Nine-Patch block.

2. Cut four (2½") squares from one of the clothing items and five (2½") squares from the second clothing item.

3. Arrange and join three of the squares to make a row referring to Figure 6; press seams toward the darker fabric square.

Figure 6

4. Repeat step 3 to make two more rows referring to Figure 7.

5. Join the rows, again referring to Figure 7 to make one version of the Nine-Patch block; press seams in one direction.

6. Repeat steps 1–5 to complete a total of five Nine-Patch blocks, creating both types of blocks as shown in Figure 5.

7. Place these blocks into the blank spaces of your arrangement.

Making Crazy-Patch Blocks

Crazy patchwork uses lots of scraps. You may cut any size shape you wish for your crazy patchwork blocks. The sample uses geometric pieces with straight sides rather than a variety of unusual shapes. These pieces are joined and then trimmed to size.

1. Select clothing items from which to cut shapes. Using a rotary cutter and ruler, cut these items into rectangles, squares or triangles.

2. Referring to Figure 8, select two pieces and sew them together on one edge; press seam open. Trim excess. Add another shape to the stitched shape, press and trim.

Figure 8

3. Continue this process until you have made a block at least 7" on each side. Trim the stitched unit to 6½" x 6½" to complete one Crazy-Patch block as shown in Figure 9.

Figure 9

4. Repeat steps 2 and 3 to complete a variety of Crazy-Patch blocks (sample uses five of these blocks).

5. Place these blocks into the blank spaces of your arrangement.

Completing the Quilt

1. Stand back and inspect your arrangement. If you like it the way it is, you are ready to join the pieces in rows and then join the rows to complete the quilt center. If you need to move the blocks around, make more blocks or replace some blocks you don't like, now is the time to make those decisions.

2. As you join the pieces in rows, press seams toward the sashing strips in the block rows and toward the sashing strips in the sashing rows.

3. Prepare 4½"-wide border strips referring to page 12 of Know the Basics and sew to the quilt edges referring to the Assembly Diagram.

4. Layer, quilt and bind edges referring to pages 12 and 13 of Know the Basics to finish the quilt. ■

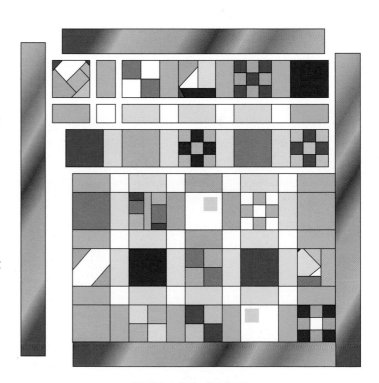

Clothing Sampler Quilt
Assembly Diagram 50" x 50"

Fussy Cutting

The quilting term "fussy-cut" refers to selectively cutting fabric to create patch/unit shapes that showcase a particular motif or part of the fabric pattern.

1. To make a fussy-cutting template, you will need a piece of cardstock, cardboard or frosted plastic template material 2" larger all around than the size of the finished fussy-cut shape. If the fussy-cut finished piece is 4" square, you will need a piece of template material at least 6" square.

2. Draw the size of the finished fussy-cut shape onto the template material, then add a 1" border all the way around.

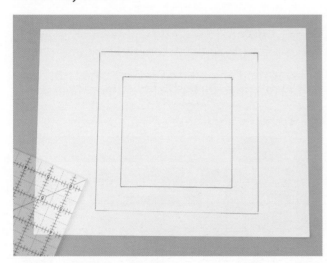

3. Cut out the center fussy-cut shape so you have a viewing window template the finished size of the patch/unit needed.

4. Use this window to audition areas of the fabric to make sure they will fit within the finished shape size and not disappear into the seams.

5. When you are happy with the fabric motif in the viewing window area, use a water-soluble marker to trace around the inside of the window.

6. Add a ¼" seam allowance around the traced area and cut out the shape.

Men's Clothing Memory Quilt

This project demonstrates an easy way to make a memory quilt using men's clothing. Constructed from jeans, plaid shirts and T-shirts, the straight-line design focuses the attention on the clothing. The sports-themed allover quilting pattern adds to the memories associated with the quilt. The layout is flexible so that the quilt can be made any size by either adding more rows for width or more strips to lengthen it. The strips may be cut smaller or larger depending on the size of the clothing used. The sample uses X-large and 2X-large size clothing, so there are larger areas from which to cut. The same layout could also be used if using women's or kids' clothing, but the strips can be cut in a smaller size.

Specifications
Skill Level: Beginner
Sample Quilt Size: 39" x 55½"

Materials
• Clothing items
• Backing to size
• Batting to size
• Thread
• Fusible stabilizer
• Basic sewing tools and supplies

Preparing the Clothing Items
1. Stabilize the chosen clothing items referring to page 10 of Know the Basics.

2. Cut the clothing items into strips—3½" x 19" and 3½" x 9¾" were used in the sample quilt.

Completing the Quilt
1. Arrange the strips on a flat surface or design wall. Rearrange as necessary to create a pleasing design.

2. When satisfied with the placement of the pieces, join the pieces on the short ends in vertical rows; press seams open to distribute bulk.

3. Join the rows to complete the quilt top; press seams open.

4. Layer, quilt and bind edges referring to pages 12 and 13 of Know the Basics to finish the quilt. *Note: The binding on the sample quilt was made using strips cut from the clothing items.* ∎

© MASTERPIECE QUILTING

Here's a Tip

Before sewing the strips together, stand back and take a good look at the layout. Ask yourself some critical design questions:

- *Do the colors balance?*
- *Do I have two pieces of the same fabric touching each other?*
- *Does the layout look visually appealing?*
- *How close is the layout to the target size?*
- *Do I need to add more pieces?*
- *Is something missing?*

If using denim jeans in the mix of fabrics, allow space between these pieces. Denim is heavier than other fabrics, so it should be spread out over the quilt rather than spaced closely together in one area.

If some of the shirts are thin from wear, adding stabilizer to them will help strengthen them. A second layer of stabilizer may be added if these shirts are still not a similar weight to the other shirts being used.

Men's Clothing Memory Quilt
Assembly Diagram 39" x 55½"

Rail Fence Tie Quilt

Men come in two groups—those who wear ties and those who don't. Those who do wear them always have lots; here's a way to make use of those extras your tie enthusiast doesn't wear anymore. Ties are an extension of the person and an expression of his personality. Regardless of whether the ties have whimsical or classic patterns, creating memory items from ties can be a lot of fun. This project shows how to use deconstructed ties like any other piece of fabric. Like other projects in this book, the layout is flexible, so the quilt can be made any size by either adding more rows for width or more blocks to lengthen it.

Specifications
Skill Level: Beginner
Sample Quilt Size: 31" x 37"

Materials
- Men's ties
- Fabric for borders and binding
- Backing to size
- Batting to size
- Thread
- Fusible stabilizer
- Basic sewing tools and supplies

Preparing the Ties
1. Deconstruct the ties and stabilize referring to Know the Basics, pages 7 and 10.

2. Separate ties into color groups based on what is available. ***Note:** You should have some light- and dark-color ties to provide contrast in the blocks.*

Completing the Quilt
1. Cut the ties into 2½" x 6½" strips. Each block requires one light and two dark strips.

2. Select one light and two dark strips; sew the light strip between the dark strips along the 6½" edges to complete one Rail Fence block as shown in Figure 1; press seams open to distribute bulk.

Figure 1

3. Repeat step 2 to complete the required number of Rail Fence blocks needed to complete the design. ***Note:** The sample has 20 Rail Fence blocks.*

4. Arrange the completed blocks on a design wall or flat surface referring to the Assembly Diagram. Move the blocks around to create a pleasing design. ***Note:** The sample quilt has five rows of four blocks each.*

5. When satisfied with the placement of the blocks, join the blocks in rows; press seams open.

6. Join the rows to complete the quilt center; press seams open.

7. Measure the quilt top to determine border sizes and prepare 4"-wide side border strips referring to page 12 of Know the Basics.

8. Sew the side border strips in place; press seams toward the strips.

9. Repeat steps 7 and 8 to add the top and bottom borders.

10. Layer, quilt and bind edges referring to pages 12 and 13 of Know the Basics to finish the quilt. ∎

T-Shirts, Memories & More

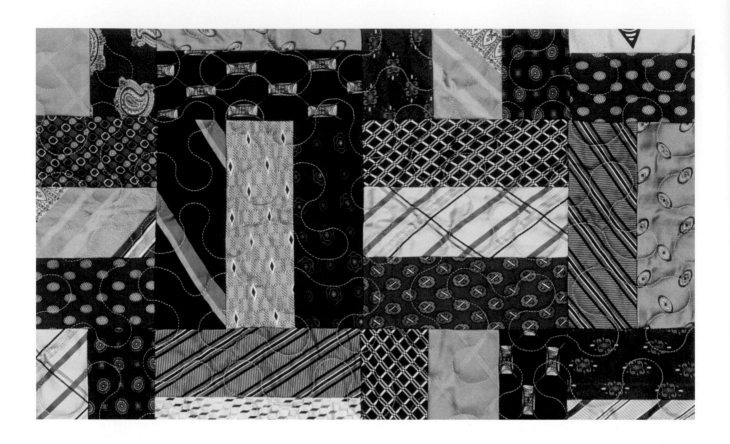

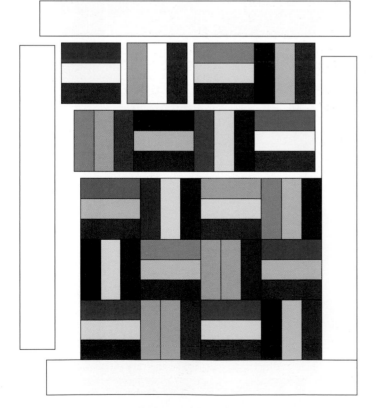

Rail Fence Tie Quilt
Assembly Diagram 31" x 37"

Here's a Tip

The Rail Fence design is created by alternating the orientation of each of the Rail Fence blocks in the rows. It can be confusing if you don't have a guide to follow. A drawing such as the Assembly Diagram will help you create the zigzagging design that is associated with this popular traditional pattern.

Crisscross Tie Block

This project uses ties that are cut into sections without deconstructing them. The sections are crisscrossed and machine-appliquéd to a background that can be made into a pillow or wall hanging. Multiple blocks may be made to create a quilt in a variety of sizes. The Placement Diagram shows a sample bed-size quilt using 16 blocks with sashing strips and squares between. These blocks may also be mixed with T-shirt, photo or other clothing blocks to create a unique memory quilt.

Specifications
Skill Level: Beginner
Sample Block Size: 16½" x 16½" unfinished

Materials
- Men's ties (3 used for each block in the sample)
- Fabric for block background
- Thread
- Basic sewing tools and supplies

Completing the Block
1. Cut the tie or ties into several sections. The sample shown uses three tie sections. The sections are cut from three different ties.

2. Cut an 18" x 18" background square. A smaller square would not have enough room to showcase the ties with any background showing.

3. Arrange the tie sections on the square with the pointed ends on the background and crisscrossing as desired referring to Figure 1 and photo. ***Note: Keep points of tie sections within the center 16"-square area of background square.***

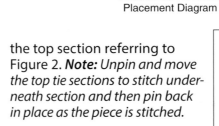
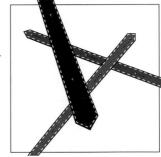

Figure 1

4. When satisfied with the positioning of the tie sections, pin to hold in place.

5. Select thread to match the tie sections and machine-topstitch the sections in place close to the edges. Start with the underneath tie section first, flipping back top sections as needed, and end with

the top section referring to Figure 2. ***Note: Unpin and move the top tie sections to stitch underneath section and then pin back in place as the piece is stitched.***

6. Trim the stitched tie block to 16½" square to complete. ■

Figure 2

Crisscross Tie Block
Placement Diagram

Irish Chain Photo Quilt

Combine Irish Chain blocks made with two colors with photos printed on fabric to showcase special memories. The size of the project depends on the number of fabric photos you have. You could combine fabric photos with T-shirts or other clothing items to create the size memory quilt you desire for a special occasion. For example, photos from a vacation could be combined with T-shirts and other cut clothing pieces purchased during that vacation.

Specifications
Skill Level: Beginner
Sample Quilt Size: 60½" x 60½"

Materials
- 24 photos printed on fabric
- Light fabric for Irish Chain blocks
- Dark fabric for Irish Chain blocks
- Dark fabric for borders and binding
- Backing to size
- Batting to size
- Thread
- Basic sewing tools and supplies

Preparing Photos
1. Prepare and print photos on fabric referring to the photo fabric manufacturer's instructions and Know the Basics on page 10.

2. To complete this project, trim the prepared fabric photos to 8" x 8".

Completing the Irish Chain Blocks
The sample quilt uses 25 Irish Chain blocks that finish at 7½" square. The sample uses a light blue for the light fabric and a dark blue for the dark fabric. The instructions given below give sizes to cut to construct one block. If making multiple blocks, refer to Completing Multiple Blocks With Strip-Pieced Units on page 50.

1. To complete one Irish Chain block, cut the following: one 3" square and eight 1¾" squares from dark fabric, and four 1¾" x 3" rectangles and four 1¾" x 5½" rectangles from light fabric.

2. Sew a 1¾" x 3" light rectangle to opposite sides of the 3" x 3" dark square to make the center row referring to Figure 1; press seams toward the dark square.

Figure 1

3. Sew a 1¾" dark square to each end of a 1¾" x 3" light rectangle to make the top row referring to Figure 2; press seams toward the dark squares. Repeat to make the bottom row.

Make 2

Figure 2

4. Sew the top and bottom rows to the center row to complete the block center referring to Figure 3; press seams toward the center row.

Figure 3

5. Sew a 1¾" x 5½" light rectangle to opposite sides of the block center referring to Figure 4; press seams toward the rectangles.

Figure 4

6. Sew a 1¾" dark square to each end of the remaining 1¾" x 5½" light rectangles to make the top and bottom rows. Sew these rows to the top and bottom of the pieced unit to complete one Irish Chain block referring to Figure 5; press seams away from the pieced unit.

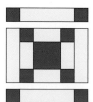

Figure 5

7. Repeat all steps to complete the number of blocks required for your quilt (25 in the sample).

Completing the Quilt

1. Arrange the Irish Chain blocks with the fabric photo blocks in seven rows of seven blocks each, alternating the placement of the blocks in the rows to create the pattern, referring to the sample photo and Assembly Diagram.

2. When you are satisfied with the arrangement, join the blocks in rows; press seams toward the fabric photo blocks.

3. Join the pieced rows to complete the quilt center; press seams in one direction.

4. Measure the quilt top to determine border sizes and prepare 4½"-wide side border strips referring to page 12 of Know the Basics.

5. Sew the side border strips in place; press seams toward the strips.

6. Repeat steps 4 and 5 to add top and bottom border strips.

7. Layer, quilt and bind edges referring to pages 12 and 13 of Know the Basics to finish the quilt. ∎

Completing Multiple Blocks With Strip-Pieced Units

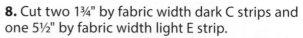

When making multiple Irish Chain blocks, it is easier and more accurate to use units that are cut from pieced strips. To make 25 Irish Chain blocks like those used in the sample quilt, you may want to try the following method.

1. Cut one 3" by fabric width dark A strip.

2. Cut two 1¾" by fabric width light B strips.

3. Sew the A strip between the two B strips along the length to make an A/B strip set; press seams toward A.

4. Subcut the A/B strip set into 3" x 5½" A-B segments as shown in Figure A. *Note: You will need two A/B strip sets to make 25 Irish Chain blocks.*

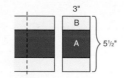

Figure A

5. Cut two 1¾" by fabric width dark C strips and one 3" by fabric width light D strip.

6. Sew the D strip between the two C strips along the length to make a C/D strip set; press seams toward C.

7. Subcut the C/D strip set into 1¾" x 5½" C-D segments as shown in Figure B. *Note: You will need three C/D strip sets to make 25 Irish Chain blocks.*

Figure B

8. Cut two 1¾" by fabric width dark C strips and one 5½" by fabric width light E strip.

9. Sew the E strip between the two C strips along the length to make a C/E strip set.

10. Subcut the C/E strip set into 1¾" x 8" C-E segments as shown in Figure C. *Note: You will need three C/E strip sets to make 25 Irish Chain blocks.*

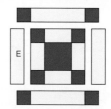

Figure C

11. Cut two 1¾" x 5½" light E rectangles to combine with the segments as shown in Figure D to complete one Irish Chain block. Repeat to make the required number of blocks.

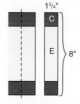

Figure D

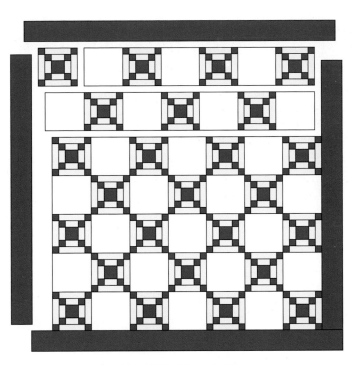

Irish Chain Photo Quilt
Assembly Diagram 60½" x 60½"

Wonky Layout Photo Quilt

The sample project will fit perfectly into the sports fan's man cave. The photos were taken at the Indianapolis Colts training camp and preseason game, and the fabrics match the team colors. The wonky layout is what makes this project extra special. The angled cut of the blocks turns average into extraordinary. The wonky layout will work with any photo theme—family, vacation, wedding and more. It can also be used with T-shirts. The sample quilt has all the blocks cut at the same angle. For variety you can change the angle to make it even wonkier.

Specifications
Skill Level: Intermediate
Sample Quilt Size: 28½" x 34"

Materials
- 12 photos printed on fabric
- Light and dark fabrics for piecing blocks and border
- Backing to size
- Batting to size
- Thread
- Basic sewing tools and supplies

Preparing Photos
1. Prepare and print photos on fabric referring to the photo fabric manufacturer's instructions and Know the Basics on page 10. **Note:** *All of the photos have the same orientation.*

2. To complete this project, trim the photos leaving ¼" beyond the edge of the photo for seam allowance. Photos do not have to be exactly the same size, but in this configuration, they should be similar in size and orientation.

Creating Wonky Photo Blocks
To create the wonky look, strips will be added around the photos and then the pieced sections are cut at an angle. The sample used 1½"-wide white strips and 2½"-wide blue strips. When combined with the photo and trimmed, the blocks finish at 9½" x 8". If you want larger blocks to accommodate larger photos, cut the darker strip wider to allow more for trimming.

1. Sew a 1½"-wide light strip to a 2½"-wide dark strip along the length to make a strip set; press seam toward the dark strip.

2. Measure the right edge of the photo and cut a strip this length plus at least 3½" (the width of the strip set).

3. With the light fabric against the photo rectangle and matching the bottom end of the rectangle to the strip, sew the strip to the rectangle, stopping stitching at least ½" from the opposite end of the rectangle to make a partial seam as shown in Figure 1; press seam toward the strip.

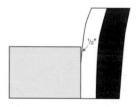

Figure 1

4. Measure the bottom edge of the photo rectangle plus the strip and cut a strip from the strip set this length. Sew the strip to the bottom edge of the photo unit with the light strip against the photo unit as shown in Figure 2; press seam toward the strip.

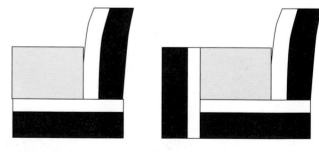

Figure 2   **Figure 3**

5. Repeat step 4 on the left edge of the photo unit to add a third section of the strip set to the photo unit as shown in Figure 3.

2013 Indianapolis Colts

2013 Indianapolis Colts

6. Fold back the excess of the beginning strip to move out of the way; measure and cut a strip that measures the width of the photo unit plus the width of the strip set or longer as shown in Figure 4.

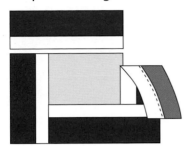

Figure 4

7. With the light strip closest to the photo unit, sew the strip to the top edge of the unit, keeping the folded beginning strip out of the way as shown in Figure 5; press seam toward the photo unit.

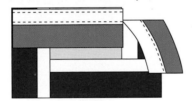

Figure 5

Wonky Layout Photo Quilt
Assembly Diagram 28½" x 34"

8. Fold the beginning strip back up and complete the seam along the unstitched edge to complete the partial seam as shown in Figure 6; press seam toward the strip.

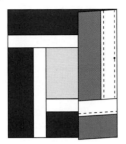

Figure 6

9. Trim any excess strip set to square up edges of the block. Trim blocks to a consistent size, if necessary.

10. To cut the block at consistent angles, lay the block on a cutting mat. Align one edge of a rotary ruler with the bottom right corner of the block and the top edge ¾" away from the seam between the light strip and the dark strip as shown in Figure 7.

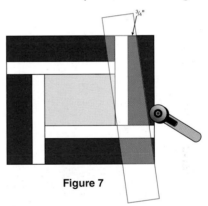

Figure 7

11. Using a rotary cutter, cut along the edge of the ruler to cut the excess away from the block to create an angle on one side of the block, again referring to Figure 7.

Here's a Tip

If your photos highlight a specific event or series of events, you might want to make a label to add to the front or back of the quilt. This is easy to make by printing text onto photo fabric referring to the product manufacturer's instructions. The label can then be appliquéd in place where desired on the quilt.

12. Turn the block so the bottom edge is next to be cut and repeat steps 10 and 11 as shown in Figure 8.

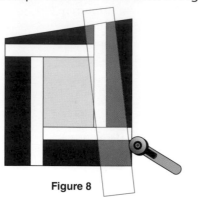

Figure 8

13. Repeat steps 10 and 11 on the remaining side and the top of the block to complete the trimming.

14. Repeat steps 1–13 to complete the desired number of blocks.

Completing the Project

1. Arrange the blocks in rows on a design wall or flat surface. Rearrange as necessary. When satisfied with the arrangement, join the blocks in four rows of three blocks each; press seams open to distribute bulk.

2. Join the rows; press.

3. A pieced border may be added to the bottom to complete the quilt top. Measure width of quilt top and piece border as desired; add to bottom of quilt top and press seam toward border.

4. Layer, quilt and bind edges referring to pages 12 and 13 of Know the Basics to finish the quilt. ∎

Scrapbook-Style Photo Layout

Preserve memories in scrapbook style to make a unique quilt. For those who are comfortable with scrapbook-style layouts, this will be very familiar. The sample project contains not only photos printed on fabric but also other memory items—in this case a man's handwritten poetry and a woman's recipe cards. Anything that can be scanned and printed is fair game to include in memory quilts! The goal was to preserve the memories of this couple, their handwriting and their passions—poetry, cooking and crocheting. The small hand-crocheted doily was added as an embellishment after quilting. The finished piece was mounted on artist canvas and framed in a vintage wood frame so it could hang on the wall as an art piece. Another option includes using the same techniques to create a pillow or a block to be pieced into a memory quilt.

Specifications
Skill Level: Intermediate
Sample Quilt Size: 16" x 20"

Materials
- Photos printed on fabric, including scanned memorabilia
- Embellishments
- Fabric for background (⅔ yard for sample size)
- Accent fabrics for layering the photos
- Lining fabric
- Batting to size
- Thread
- Artist canvas
- Wood frame with glass removed to fit project
- Basic sewing tools and supplies

Preparing the Background
1. To make a project similar to the sample, cut a piece of background fabric 20" x 24". This is cut larger than the finished top to allow extra fabric for mounting on the frame.

2. Fold the background rectangle in quarters and crease to mark the horizontal and vertical centers. Place a pin at each crease or use a water-erasable marker to mark these centerlines referring to Figure 1.

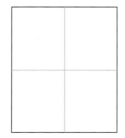

Figure 1

3. Using pins or a water-erasable marker, mark 16" x 20" boundary lines on the background, centering the lines as shown in Figure 2.

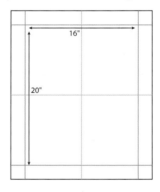

Figure 2

Preparing Memory Items
1. Prepare and print photos and other memorabilia on fabric referring to the photo fabric manufacturer's instructions and Know the Basics on page 10.

2. To complete this project, trim the fabric photos or other printed items leaving at least ¼" beyond the printed edge for the seam allowance.

3. For all printed items that are to be framed, fold the seam allowance to the wrong side all around and press to hold.

4. If using accent fabric under an item, cut a piece of accent fabric at least 1¼" larger than the item all around. For example, if your pressed item is 4" x 6", cut a 6½" x 8½" accent rectangle to go with it to provide a seam allowance to turn under and a border around the memory item.

5. Center and pin the memory item to the right side of the pressed accent rectangle referring to Figure 3.

Figure 3

6. Using thread to match and a machine appliqué stitch, sew the memory item to the accent rectangle all around (Photo 1).

Photo 1

7. Repeat steps 3–6 with other memory items to be framed.

8. If some memory items are not being framed, turn the seam allowance to the wrong side, press and baste to hold in place until ready to attach to the background.

Completing the Fabric Scrapbook

1. Lay the marked background rectangle on a flat surface or place on a design wall.

2. Fold the edges of each accent fabric to the wrong side ¼" and press to hold (Photo 2).

Photo 2

3. Pin memory items in place using string as a guide to keep the items within the size of the frame referring to Photo 3 for placement suggestions.

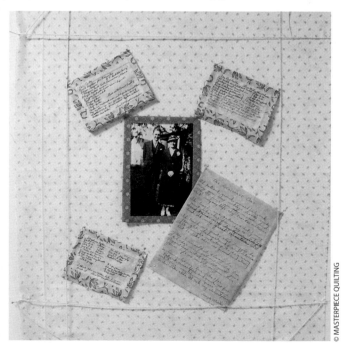

Photo 3

4. Using thread to match and a machine appliqué stitch, sew the memory items to the background rectangle.

Here's a Tip

If layering items, sew the bottom item on first and then layer the other item on top and sew to the background last. You may leave the area under the layered item unstitched. It can also be trimmed away if the layers create excess bulk under the top layered item.

5. Layer the completed top with batting and lining and quilt within the marked boundaries but not over the memory items. ***Note:*** *On the sample, the memory items were outlined by machine, and the background was quilted in straight lines from top to bottom ½" apart.*

6. Hand-stitch other embellishments in place at this time. ***Note:*** *The crocheted doily was added to the sample at this time (Photo 4).*

Photo 4

7. Mount the completed top on the artist canvas and insert in a frame to finish. ■

Scrapbook-Style Photo Layout
Placement Diagram 16" x 20"

T-Shirt Pillow

Preserve childhood T-shirts in a pillow with the addition of a novelty fabric and a wonky-style backing. This project serves as an excellent example of how a novelty fabric such as the John Deere tractor print can be incorporated in a project to complement the theme of a few T-shirts.

Specifications
Skill Level: Beginner
Sample Pillow Size: 18" x 18"

Materials
- T-shirts for pillow top
- Fabric for piecing the pillow top
- Lining fabric for pillow top
- Backing to size (T-shirts used in sample)
- Batting to size
- Thread
- Fusible stabilizer
- Pillow form to fit finished pillow
- Basic sewing tools and supplies

Completing the Pillow Top

1. Prepare T-shirts with fusible stabilizer as directed on page 10 of the Know the Basics section. Three T-shirts were used in the sample pillow.

2. Trim the prepared T-shirts to within 3" of the logos all around.

3. Create a rough layout of the pillow top using the sizes of the T-shirt logos to determine placement. In the sample, one T-shirt was turned with the logo sideways and combined with two other T-shirts with the logos upright as shown in the photo.

4. Refer to the Planning the Layout sidebar on page 64 for more information about planning, bordering and joining the T-shirt logos to complete the pillow top.

5. Cut batting and lining squares larger than the completed pillow top all around.

6. Sandwich the batting between the pillow top and the lining square; pin or baste layers to hold together.

7. Quilt as desired by hand or machine; remove pins or basting when quilting is complete.

8. Trim the quilted pillow top to 18½" x 18½".

Completing the Pillow

1. To make the pillow backing, stabilize 20" squares cut from two T-shirts that will coordinate with the pillow top. ***Note:*** *The sample uses green and yellow T-shirt strips that match the accent colors in the T-shirt logos and the novelty print used as borders on the pillow top.*

2. Cut 20"-long strips with a slight angle from the stabilized T-shirt squares. The strips can be 1½"–2½" wide at one end and 2½"–3½" wide at the other end as shown in Figure 1.

1½"–2½"

2½"–3½"

Figure 1

3. Join the strips, alternating the colors and angles to make a large square as shown in Figure 2; press seams open.

Figure 2

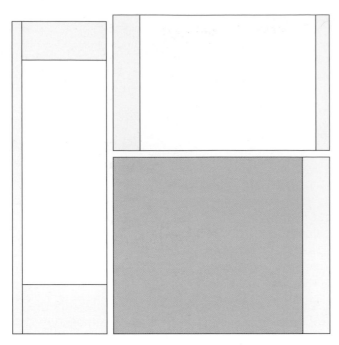

T-Shirt Pillow
Assembly Diagram 18" x 18"

4. Measure and trim the pieced section to 18½" x 18½".

5. Place the pillow back right sides together with the pillow top and stitch layers together all around, leaving an 8" opening on one side. Secure seam at beginning and end.

6. Trim corners to reduce bulk. Turn the pillow cover right side out through the opening and press edges flat. Poke out corners using the eraser end of a pencil or similar object to make them square.

7. Press pillow cover edges to flatten seams. Press the opening edges to the inside ¼".

8. Insert pillow form through the opening.

9. Hand-stitch the opening closed along the previously pressed edges to finish. ∎

Planning the Layout

After you have prepared and trimmed the T-shirts to within 3" of the logos, it's time to figure out how your pillow top will be configured. A sketch will help you figure it out. Draft a rough sketch on paper, adding the sizes of the T-shirt blocks to the drawing. Knowing the target size before finishing helps you determine the layout of the pillow.

Place the T-shirt blocks on a flat surface, referencing your rough sketch. Ask yourself some critical design questions:

• Do the colors balance?
• Does the layout look visually appealing?
• How close is the layout to the target size?
• Is anything missing?

The unquilted pillow top should measure at least 19" square so it can be trimmed to 18½" square after quilting. If using only three T-shirts as in the sample, additional fabric will be needed to fill in and balance the layout.

Select a fabric that will complement the colors of the T-shirt blocks. In the sample, a yellow background novelty fabric was used because each of the T-shirt blocks had yellow accents. The yellow novelty print brings out those yellow accents and balances the color placement.

Cut strips of the novelty fabric and border the T-shirt blocks, pressing the seams toward the strips after stitching. Continue to add fabric strips of the novelty print until the units will fit together.

Join the stitched units. If the pillow top is not at least 19" square, add borders around outer edges to add to the size.

Complete the pillow referring to the instructions after the pillow top has been pieced.

Dresden Plate Tie Pillow

This project incorporates men's ties along with a button-front shirt into a memory pillow.

This can be a very effective way to use professional dress attire from a businessman to create

multiple memory items that are similar so several family members can share in the memories.

The Dresden Plate is a classic quilt pattern, and it adds a touch of elegance to a pillow.

Specifications
Skill Level: Confident Beginner
Sample Pillow Size: 18" x 18"

Materials
- 1 men's button-front shirt
- 5 different men's ties
- Fabric for background squares (⅓ yard used in sample)
- Lining fabric for pillow top
- Batting to size
- Thread
- Fusible stabilizer
- Pillow form
- Template material
- Basic sewing tools and supplies

Completing the Pillow Top
The size of this pillow is dependent upon the size of the men's dress shirt. The pillow back is made from the front of the button-front shirt, so the shirt's size determines how large the pillow can be made. Most men's shirts that are size Large or larger will yield a 20" square. Smaller shirts or those with a tailored fit may not.

With the buttons buttoned, lay the shirt flat and measure from side seam to side along the seam at the bottom and also from armpit to armpit. Measure the distance from the bottom of the button placket up to an imaginary line across the narrowest point of the armhole. Using these measurements, you can determine what size pillow form you will need and what size pillow you can create.

For designing and construction, add at least 2" to the size pillow you can make to allow for shrinkage during quilting and squaring up the pillow top after quilting.

1. Deconstruct the ties as directed on page 7 of Know the Basics section and add stabilizer.

2. Trace the Dresden pattern given on page 69 onto the template material and cut out to make a template.

3. Trace the template shape onto the wrong side of the prepared ties, tracing four on each tie. Cut out shapes on traced lines to make a total of 20 Dresden pieces.

4. Press ¼" to the wrong side on each side of the pointed end of each Dresden shape as shown in Figure 1.

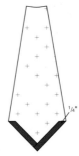

Figure 1

5. Select one Dresden shape from each tie to total five different-color shapes; arrange in a pleasing order as shown in Figure 2.

Figure 2   **Figure 3**

6. Join the Dresden shapes as arranged using a ¼" seam allowance to make a quarter unit as shown in Figure 3; press seams open to distribute bulk.

7. Repeat steps 5 and 6 to make a total of four identical quarter units.

8. Cut the background fabric into four 10½" squares.

9. Place a quarter unit on each square, aligning the straight edges referring to Figure 4; pin or baste in place to hold.

Figure 4

10. Appliqué the turned-under edges of the quarter units in place by hand or machine. **Note:** *A machine appliqué stitch was used to stitch the sample pieces in place.*

11. Arrange the appliquéd block quarters in two rows of two block quarters each; join in rows and then join the rows to complete the Dresden block as shown in Figure 5; press seams open.

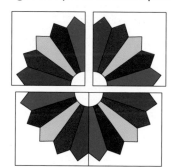

Figure 5

12. Select a 4½" square of a tie section and cut a 4" circle from the square. Prepare the circle and appliqué in place in the center of the Dresden block referring to Preparing Perfect Circles With Seam Allowance for Appliqué on page 69.

13. Cut batting and lining squares larger than the completed Dresden block pillow top all around.

14. Sandwich the batting between the pillow top and the lining square; pin or baste layers to hold together.

15. Quilt as desired by hand or machine; remove pins or basting when quilting is complete.

16. Trim the quilted pillow top to 18½" x 18½".

Completing the Pillow

1. Prepare the pillow backing using the front of the button-front shirt referring to pages 9 and 10 of Know the Basics.

2. Unbutton several buttons on the shirt backing section. Place the pillow back right sides together with the pillow top and stitch layers together all around.

3. Trim corners to reduce bulk. Turn the pillow cover right side out through the open button section. Poke out corners using the eraser end of a pencil or similar object to make them square.

Dresden Plate Tie Pillow
Placement Diagram 18" x 18"

4. Press pillow cover edges to flatten seams.

5. Insert pillow form through the opening.

6. Button up shirt opening to finish. ∎

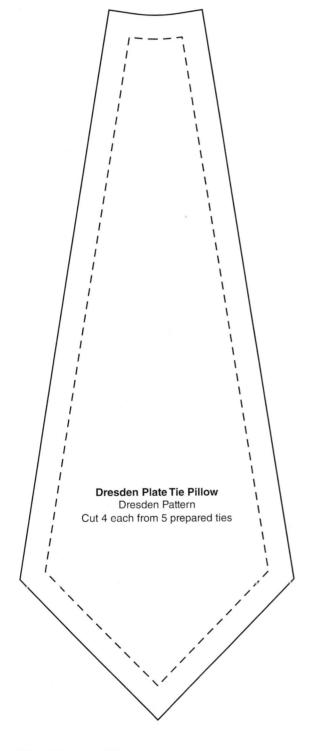

Dresden Plate Tie Pillow
Dresden Pattern
Cut 4 each from 5 prepared ties

Preparing Perfect Circles With Seam Allowance for Appliqué

Method 1

Pin a finished-size freezer-paper circle, shiny side up, to wrong side of fabric; trim seam allowance to ⅛". Carefully press the allowance over the freezer paper with a hot iron, creating small pleats as shown in Figure A.

Figure A

Method 2

Machine-stitch around the outside edge of the uncut traced fabric circle. Place a desired-size cardstock circle in the center of the stitched circle and draw up the fabric, yo-yo style, as shown in Figure B. Make a knot; press. Remove the cardstock circle before appliquéing to the background.

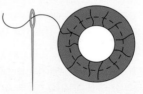

Figure B

Method 3

Similar to Method 1, but done by hand, this method works well when making small circles as well as larger ones. Put a finished-size cardstock circle in the center of the circle of fabric, stitch a line of hand-sewn gathering stitches around the edges of the cardstock circle and pull to gather the edge fabric around the cardstock circle as shown in Figure C. Make a knot; press. Remove the cardstock circle before appliquéing to the background.

Figure C

Wedding Dress Pillow

This project is a stylish way to commemorate a couple's special day. It features a wedding photo along with bridal satin and an accent stripe. The sample is quilted in a contemporary style to match the couple. This is a perfect gift for a first wedding anniversary! This type of pillow project would be a neat way to "share" an ancestor's vintage wedding dress with several family members too. Embellishments would be perfect for this pillow. Another option is to use this layout, and instead of making a pillow, insert the block into a memory quilt.

Specifications
Skill Level: Intermediate
Sample Pillow Size: 18" x 18"

Materials
- Fabric photo
- Fabric for piecing pillow top and accents (satin and cotton used in sample)
- Lining fabric for pillow top
- Batting to size
- Thread
- Pillow form
- Basic sewing tools and supplies

Completing the Pillow Top
1. Prepare and print photo on fabric referring to the photo fabric manufacturer's instructions and Know the Basics on page 10.

2. To complete this project, trim the photo leaving ¼" beyond the edge of the photo for seam allowance.

Here's a Tip

Satin fabrics are more fragile than cotton. Test your iron on a scrap before ironing on the pieces being used in the pillow. If you find there is a problem with pressing, use a pressing cloth and keep your iron from touching the satin fabric.

Satin will fray during handling. You may need to sew a zigzag stitch along each edge of the fabric to reduce raveling during construction and use.

3. On a piece of sketch paper or graph paper, draw out the finished pillow top, adding in the measurements of the fabric photo and the desired size of your finished pillow.

4. Calculate the width of the pieces bordering the photo and cut out, adding ½" to finished sizes for seam allowance.

5. To assemble the pillow, sew a narrow accent strip between two narrow satin strips to make a pieced side strip as shown in Figure 1; press seams toward the accent strip. Repeat to make a second pieced strip.

Figure 1

6. Stitch pieced strips to prepared fabric photo using the partial seam techniques in Wonky Layout Photo Quilt on page 52. Refer to Figure 2 to add a pieced strip to the right edge of the prepared fabric photo, except align the first strip with the top edge of the photo and work in the opposite direction from that shown in Wonky Layout Photo Quilt to add strips.

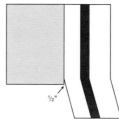

Figure 2

7. Add the remaining pieced and unpieced strips to the fabric photo referring to Wonky Layout Photo Quilt to finish the pieced pillow top referring to Figure 3 and the photo below.

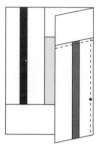

Figure 3

8. Cut batting and lining squares larger than the completed pillow top all around.

9. Sandwich the batting between the pillow top and the lining square; pin or baste layers to hold together.

10. Quilt as desired by hand or machine; remove pins or basting when quilting is complete.

11. Trim the quilted pillow top to 18½" x 18½".

Completing the Pillow

1. Cut an 18½" x 18½" backing square.

2. Place the pillow back right sides together with the pillow top and stitch layers together all around, leaving an 8" opening on one side. Secure seam at beginning and end.

3. Trim corners to reduce bulk. Turn the pillow cover right side out through the opening and press edges flat. Poke out corners using the eraser end of a pencil or similar object to make them square.

4. Press pillow cover edges to flatten seams. Press the opening edges to the inside ¼".

5. Insert pillow form through the opening.

6. Hand-stitch the opening closed along the previously pressed edges to finish. ∎

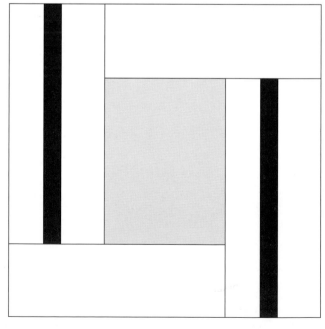

Wedding Dress Pillow
Placement Diagram 18" x 18"

The Gallery

Boggs Anniversary Photo Quilt
COURTESY OF CAROLYN BOGGS
DESIGNED AND QUILTED BY NANCY SCOTT

This wall hanging was commissioned as a 60th wedding anniversary gift. The gray fabric was used to match the decor of the couple's home, and the size was limited by available wall space in their living room. The photos were arranged in rows with the center being arranged in more of a cluster style.

74

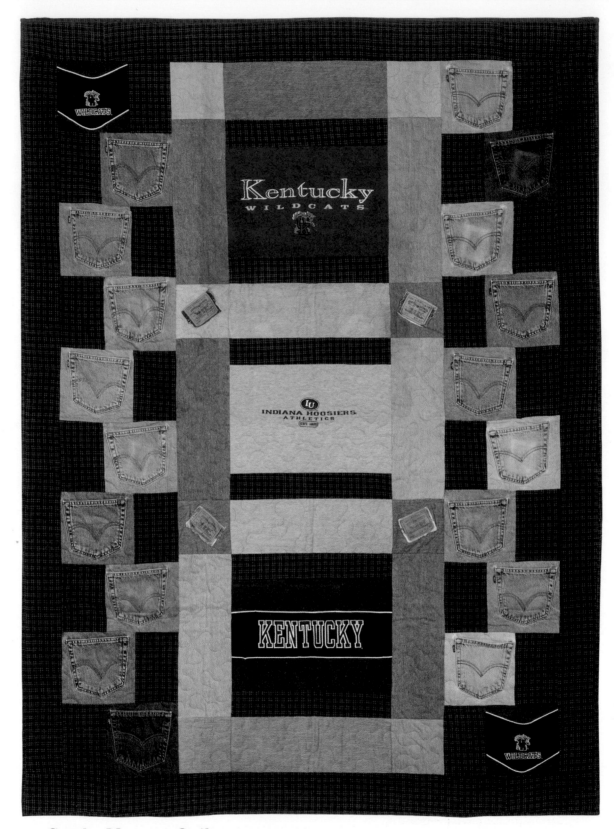

Combs Memory Quilt

COURTESY OF CHERYL COMBS

DESIGNED AND QUILTED BY NANCY SCOTT

This memory quilt incorporated the jeans and shirts from a deceased husband. The pockets were kept open so that the widow could tuck her hands into them as she cuddled with the blanket.

Jayde's T-Shirt Quilt

COURTESY OF JAYDE SILLS

DESIGNED AND QUILTED BY NANCY SCOTT

This quilt was made in honor of a high school graduation. As a very active person, Jayde had a lot of T-shirts to fit into a full-size quilt to take to college with her. The shirts were trimmed close to the logos, and a cluster layout was used for the top and bottom rows to get all the shirts to fit. The center section was arranged into columns with vertical sashing. A bright, colorful batik was selected for the sashing and borders, which matched her personality and provided a unified look to the quilt.

Keepsake Harley Davidson Quilt

COURTESY OF KEEPSAKE THREADS

DESIGN BY KEEPSAKE THREADS

QUILTED BY NANCY SCOTT

The framing technique is featured on each of the T-shirts through the use of black horizontal and vertical sashing. This quilt includes novelty fabrics for border and appliqué flames.

Keepsake Threads Tie Memory Quilt
COURTESY OF KEEPSAKE THREADS
DESIGN BY KEEPSAKE THREADS
QUILTED BY NANCY SCOTT

The blocks show ties in a crisscross wonky style. This quilt features thin sashing and a minimalistic border for a very contemporary look.

Kiss Quilt
COURTESY OF JORDAN MILLER
DESIGNED AND QUILTED BY LINDA BUSHEE CUSTOM QUILTS

A more advanced layout, incorporating pieced blocks in addition to sashing around the T-shirts, is shown on this quilt made up of a variety of logo shapes.

Patriotic Quilt

COURTESY OF NANCY SCOTT

DESIGNED AND QUILTED BY NANCY SCOTT

This was the first T-shirt quilt Nancy Scott made when she started her longarm quilting business in 2007. The horizontal rows are different sizes and are separated by vertical sashing. Within each row, the horizontal sashes are cut at slightly different widths. Novelty fabrics are incorporated to support the patriotic theme.

Tyler Ulmer T-Shirt Quilt

COURTESY OF TYLER ULMER

DESIGNED AND QUILTED BY LINDA BUSHEE CUSTOM QUILTS

A favorite color of orange is featured in this quilt that shows a more advanced layout. The T-shirts are sashed and are also surrounded by pieced blocks.

Special Thanks

To all of my customers for allowing me to use their quilts for photos in this book—Nancy

Bosal #300 Fashion Fuse Woven Stabilizer
Bosal Foam & Fiber
171 Washington St.
Limerick, ME 04048
(800) 343-1818

T-Shirts, Memories & More is published by Annie's, 306 East Parr Road, Berne, IN 46711. Printed in USA. Copyright © 2014 Annie's. All rights reserved. This publication may not be reproduced in part or in whole without written permission from the publisher.

RETAIL STORES: If you would like to carry this pattern book or any other Annie's publication, visit AnniesWSL.com.

Every effort has been made to ensure that the instructions in this pattern book are complete and accurate. We cannot, however, take responsibility for human error, typographical mistakes or variations in individual work. Please visit AnniesCustomerCare.com to check for pattern updates.

Library of Congress Control Number: 2013921794
ISBN: 978-1-57367-377-8
2 3 4 5 6 7 8 9